History & Geography 800
Teacher's Guide

CONTENTS

Author: **Theresa Buskey, B.A., J.D.**

Editor: Alan Christopherson, M.S.

Alpha Omega Publications®

804 N. 2nd Ave. E., Rock Rapids, IA 51246-1759

CVERVIEW

HISTORY & GEOGRAPHY

■━━━━━━━━━━━━━━━━━━━━━━━━━■

Curriculum Overview
Grades 1–12

History & Geography LIFEPAC Overview

	Grade 1	Grade 2	Grade 3
LIFEPAC 1	**I AM A SPECIAL PERSON** • God made me • You are God's child • All about you • Using proper manners	**FAMILIES AND NEIGHBORS** • We need a family • We help our family • Our neighborhood • Helping our neighbors	**FISHING IN MAINE** • At look at Deer Island • A lobster boat • Planting lobster traps • Catching lobsters
LIFEPAC 2	**COMMUNICATING WITH SOUND** • Sounds people make • Sounds that communicate • Communicating without sound • Communicating with God	**COMMUNITY HELPERS** • What is a community • Community helpers • Your church community • Helping your community	**FARMING IN KANSAS** • The six parts of Kansas • Getting to know Kansas • Exploring Kansas • Harvest in Kansas
LIFEPAC 3	**I HAVE FEELINGS** • I feel sad • I feel afraid • I feel happy • I have other feelings	**NEIGHBORHOOD STORES** • Pioneer goods and services • Modern goods and services • Some business rules • God's business rules	**FRUIT-GROWING IN WASHINGTON** • Geography of Washington • Cities in Washington • Apple blossom time • Apple harvest time
LIFEPAC 4	**I LIVE IN A FAMILY** • My mother and father • My brothers and sisters • My grandparents • What my family does	**FARMS AND CITIES** • Farming long ago • Farming today • Growing cities • Changing cities	**FORESTS IN OREGON** • A land of forests • Trees of the forests • Lumbering in Oregon • Keeping Oregon's forests
LIFEPAC 5	**YOU AND GOD'S FAMILY** • Getting ready in the morning • Walking to school • The school family • The church family	**NEIGHBORS AROUND THE WORLD** • Things all families need • How communities share • How communities change • Customs of the world	**CALIFORNIA: A GOLDEN LAND** • Early California • The ranch community • A trip around the state • Work on a truck farm
LIFEPAC 6	**PLACES PEOPLE LIVE** • Life on the farm • Life in the city • Life by the sea	**A JAPANESE FAMILY** • Places people live in Japan • School in Japan • Work in Japan • Play in Japan	**CATTLE IN TEXAS** • Learning about Texas • Early ranches in Texas • Life on a ranch • A cattle round-up
LIFEPAC 7	**COMMUNITY HELPERS** • Firemen and policemen • Doctors • City workers • Teachers and ministers	**HOW WE TRAVEL** • Travel in Bible times • Travel in the past • Travel today • Changes in today's world	**COAL MINING IN PENNSYLVANIA** • The formation of coal • Products from coal • Methods of mining coal • The state of Pennsylvania
LIFEPAC 8	**I LOVE MY COUNTRY** • America discovered • The Pilgrims • The United States begin • Respect for your country	**MESSAGES FROM FAR AND NEAR** • Communication in Bible times • Communication today • Reasons for communication • Communication without sound	**MANUFACTURING IN MICHIGAN** • Facts about Michigan • Interesting people of Michigan • Places in Michigan • The treasures in Michigan
LIFEPAC 9	**I LIVE IN THE WORLD** • The globe • Countries • Friends in Mexico • Friends in Japan	**CARING FOR OUR NEIGHBORHOODS** • God's plan for nature • Sin changed nature • Problems in our neighborhoods • Helping our neighborhoods	**SPACE TRAVEL IN FLORIDA** • A place to launch spacecraft • Worker at the Space Center • The first flights • The trip to the moon
LIFEPAC 10	**THE WORLD AND YOU** • You are special • Your family • Your school and church • Your world	**PEOPLE DEPEND ON EACH OTHER** • Depending on our families • Depending on our neighbors • Depending on our communities • Communicating with God	**REVIEW OF NINE STATES** • California and Kansas • Washington and Maine • Oregon and Pennsylvania • Texas, Florida, and Michigan

Grade 4	Grade 5	Grade 6	
OUR EARTH • The surface of the earth • Early explorations of the earth • Exploring from space • Exploring the oceans	**A NEW WORLD** • Exploration of America • The first colonies • Conflict with Britain • Birth of the United States	**WORLD GEOGRAPHY** • Latitude and longitude • Western and eastern hemispheres • The southern hemisphere • Political and cultural regions	LIFEPAC 1
SEAPORT CITIES • Sydney • Hong Kong • Istanbul • London	**A NEW NATION** • War for Independence • Life in America • A new form of government • The Nation's early years	**THE CRADLE OF CIVILIZATION** • Mesopotamia • The land of Israel • The Nation of Israel • Egypt	LIFEPAC 2
DESERT LANDS • What is a desert? • Where are the deserts? • How do people live in the desert?	**A TIME OF TESTING** • Louisiana Purchase • War of 1812 • Sectionalism • Improvements in trade & travel	**GREECE AND ROME** • Geography of the region • Beginning civilizations • Contributions to other civilizations • The influence of Christianity	LIFEPAC 3
GRASSLANDS • Grasslands of the world • Ukraine • Kenya • Argentina	**A GROWING NATION** • Andrew Jackson's influence • Texas & Oregon • Mexican War • The Nation divides	**THE MIDDLE AGES** • The feudal system • Books and schools • The Crusades • Trade and architecture	LIFEPAC 4
TROPICAL RAIN FORESTS • Facts about rain forests • Rain forests of the world • The Amazon rain forest • The Congo rain forest	**A DIVIDED NATION** • Civil War • Reconstruction • Gilded Age • The need for reform	**SIX SOUTH AMERICAN COUNTRIES** • Brazil • Colombia • Venezuela • Three Guianas	LIFEPAC 5
THE POLAR REGIONS • The polar regions: coldest places in the world • The Arctic polar region • The Antarctic polar region	**A CHANGING NATION** • Progressive reforms • Spanish-American War • World War I • Roaring Twenties	**OTHER AMERICAN COUNTRIES** • Ecuador and Peru • Bolivia and Uruguay • Paraguay and Argentina • Chile	LIFEPAC 6
MOUNTAIN COUNTRIES • Peru – the Andes • The Incas and modern Peru • Nepal – the Himalayas • Switzerland – the Alps	**DEPRESSION AND WAR** • The Great Depression • War begins in Europe • War in Europe • War in the Pacific	**AFRICA** • Geography and cultures • Countries of northern Africa • Countries of central Africa • Countries of southern Africa	LIFEPAC 7
ISLAND COUNTRIES • Islands of the earth • Cuba • Iceland • Japan	**COLD WAR** • Korean War & other crises • Vietnam War • Civil Rights Movement • Upheaval in America	**MODERN WESTERN EUROPE** • The Renaissance • The Industrial Revolution • World War I • World War II	LIFEPAC 8
NORTH AMERICA • Geography • Lands, lakes and rivers • Northern countries • Southern countries	**INTO THE NEW MILLENNIUM** • Watergate and détente • The fall of Communism • The Persian Gulf War • Issues of the new millennium	**MODERN EASTERN EUROPE** • Early government • Early churches • Early countries • Modern countries	LIFEPAC 9
OUR WORLD IN REVIEW • Europe and the explorers • Asia and Africa • Southern continents • North America, North Pole	**THE UNITED STATES OF AMERICA** • Beginning America until 1830 • Stronger America 1830-1930 • 1930 to the end of the millennium • The new millennium	**THE DEVELOPMENT OF OUR WORLD** • Cradle of civilization • The Middle Ages • Modern Europe • South America and Africa	LIFEPAC 10

History & Geography LIFEPAC Overview

	Grade 7	Grade 8	Grade 9
LIFEPAC 1	**WHAT IS HISTORY** • Definition and significance of history • Historians and the historical method • Views of history	**EUROPE COMES TO AMERICA** • Voyages of Columbus • Spanish exploration • Other exploration • The first colonies	**UNITED STATES HERITAGE** • American colonies • Acquisitions and annexations • Backgrounds to freedom • Backgrounds to society
LIFEPAC 2	**WHAT IS GEOGRAPHY** • Classes of geography • Geography and relief of the earth • Maps and the study of our world • Time zones	**BRITISH AMERICA** • English colonies • Government • Lifestyle • Wars with France	**OUR NATIONAL GOVERNMENT** • Ideals of national government • National government developed • Legislative and Executive branches • Judicial branch
LIFEPAC 3	**U.S. HISTORY AND GEOGRAPHY** • Geography of the U.S. • Early history of the U.S. • Physical regions of the U.S. • Cultural regions of the U.S.	**THE AMERICAN REVOLUTION** • British control • Rebellion of the Colonies • War for independence • Constitution	**STATE AND LOCAL GOVERNMENT** • Powers of state government • County government • Township government • City government
LIFEPAC 4	**ANTHROPOLOGY** • Understanding anthropology • The unity of man • The diversity of man • The culture of man	**A FIRM FOUNDATION** • Washington's presidency • Adams administration • Jeffersonian Democracy • War of 1812	**PLANNING A CAREER** • Definition of a career • God's will concerning a career • Selecting a career • Preparation for a career
LIFEPAC 5	**SOCIOLOGY** • Sociology defined • Historical development • Importance to Christians • Method of sociology	**A GROWING NATION** • Jacksonian Era • Northern border • Southern border • Industrial Revolution	**CITIZENSHIP** • Citizenship defined • Gaining citizenship • Rights of citizenship • Responsibilities of citizenship
LIFEPAC 6	**U.S. ANTHROPOLOGY** • Cultural background of the U.S. • Native American cultures • Cultures from distant lands • Cultural and social interaction	**THE CIVIL WAR** • Division & Secession • Civil War • Death of Lincoln • Reconstruction	**THE EARTH AND MAN** • Man inhabits the earth • Man's home on the earth • Man develops the earth • The future of the earth
LIFEPAC 7	**ECONOMICS** • Economics defined • Methods of the economist • Tools of the economist • An experiment in economy	**GILDED AGE TO PROGRESSIVE ERA** • Rise of industry • Wild West • America as a world power • Progressive era	**REGIONS OF THE WORLD** • A region defined • Geographic and climate regions • Cultural and political regions • Economic regions of Europe
LIFEPAC 8	**POLITICAL SCIENCE** • Definition of political science • Roots of Western thought • Modern political thinkers • Political theory	**A WORLD IN CONFLICT** • World War I • Great Depression • New Deal • World War II	**MAN AND HIS ENVIRONMENT** • The physical environment • Drug abuse • The social environment • Man's responsibilities
LIFEPAC 9	**STATE ECONOMICS AND POLITICS** • Background of state government • State government • State finance • State politics	**COLD WAR AMERICA** • Origins of the Cold War • Vietnam • Truman to Nixon • Ending of the Cold War	**TOOLS OF THE GEOGRAPHER** • The globe • Types of maps • Reading maps • The earth in symbol form
LIFEPAC 10	**SOCIAL SCIENCES REVIEW** • History and geography • Anthropology • Sociology • Economics and politics	**RECENT AMERICA & REVIEW** • Europe to independence • Colonies to the Civil War • Civil War to World War II • World War II through Cold War	**MAN IN A CHANGING WORLD** • Development of the nation • Development of government • Development of the earth • Solving problems

Grade 10	Grade 11	Grade 12	
ANCIENT CIVILIZATION • Origin of civilization • Early Egypt • Assyria and Babylonia • Persian civilization	FOUNDATIONS OF DEMOCRACY • Democracy develops • Virginia • New England colonies • Middle and southern colonies	INTERNATIONAL GOVERNMENTS • Why have governments • Types of governments • Governments in our world • Political thinkers	LIFEPAC 1
ANCIENT CIVILIZATIONS • India • China • Greek civilization • Roman Empire	CONSTITUTIONAL GOVERNMENT • Relations with England • The Revolutionary War • Articles of Confederation • Constitution of the U.S.	UNITED STATES GOVERNMENT • U.S. Constitution • Bill of Rights • Three branches of government • Legislative process	LIFEPAC 2
THE MEDIEVAL WORLD • Introduction to Middle Ages • Early Middle Ages • Middle Ages in transition • High Middle Ages	NATIONAL EXPANSION • A strong federal government • Revolution of 1800 • War of 1812 • Nationalism and sectionalism	AMERICAN PARTY SYSTEM • American party system • Development political parties • Functions of political parties • Voting	LIFEPAC 3
RENAISSANCE AND REFORMATION • Changes in government and art • Changes in literature and thought • Advances in science • Reform within the Church	A NATION DIVIDED • Issues of division • Division of land and people • Economics of slavery • Politics of slavery	HISTORY OF GOVERNMENTS • Primitive governments • Beginnings of Democracy • Feudalism, Theocracy & Democracy • Fascism & Nazism	LIFEPAC 4
GROWTH OF WORLD EMPIRES • England and France • Portugal and Spain • Austria and Germany • Italy and the Ottoman Empire	A NATION UNITED AGAIN • Regionalism • The division • The Civil War • Reconstruction	THE CHRISTIAN & GOVERNMENT • Discrimination & the Christian • Christian attitudes • "Opinion & Truth" in politics • Politics & Propaganda	LIFEPAC 5
THE AGE OF REVOLUTION • Factors leading to revolution • The English Revolution • The American Revolution • The French Revolution	INVOLVEMENT AT HOME & ABROAD • Surge of industry • The industrial lifestyle • Isolationism • Involvement in conflict	FREE ENTERPRISE • Economics • Competition • Money through history • International finance & currency	LIFEPAC 6
THE INDUSTRIAL REVOLUTION • Sparks of preparation • Industrial revolution in England • Industrial revolution in America • Social changes of the revolution	THE SEARCH FOR PEACE • The War and its aftermath • The Golden Twenties • The Great Depression • The New Deal	BUSINESS AND YOU • Running a business • Government & business • Banks & Mergers • Deregulation & Bankruptcy	LIFEPAC 7
TWO WORLD WARS • Mounting tension • World War I • Peace and power quests • World War II	A NATION AT WAR • Causes of the war • World War II • Korean Conflict • Vietnam Conflict	THE STOCK MARKET • How it started and works • Selecting stocks • Types of stocks • Tracking stocks	LIFEPAC 8
THE CONTEMPORARY WORLD • Korean War • International organizations • Atomic stalemate • A form of coexistence	CONTEMPORARY AMERICA • America in the 1960s • America in the 1970s • America in the 1980s & 90s • International Scene 1980–Present	BUDGET AND FINANCE • Cash, Credit & Checking • Buying a car • Grants, Loans & IRAs • Savings & E-cash	LIFEPAC 9
ANCIENT TIMES TO THE PRESENT • Ancient civilizations • Medieval times • The Renaissance • The modern world	UNITED STATES HISTORY • Basis of democracy • The 1800s • Industrialization • Current history	GEOGRAPHY AND REVIEW • Euro & International finance • U.S. Geography • The global traveler • Neighbors, Heroes & The Holy Land	LIFEPAC 10

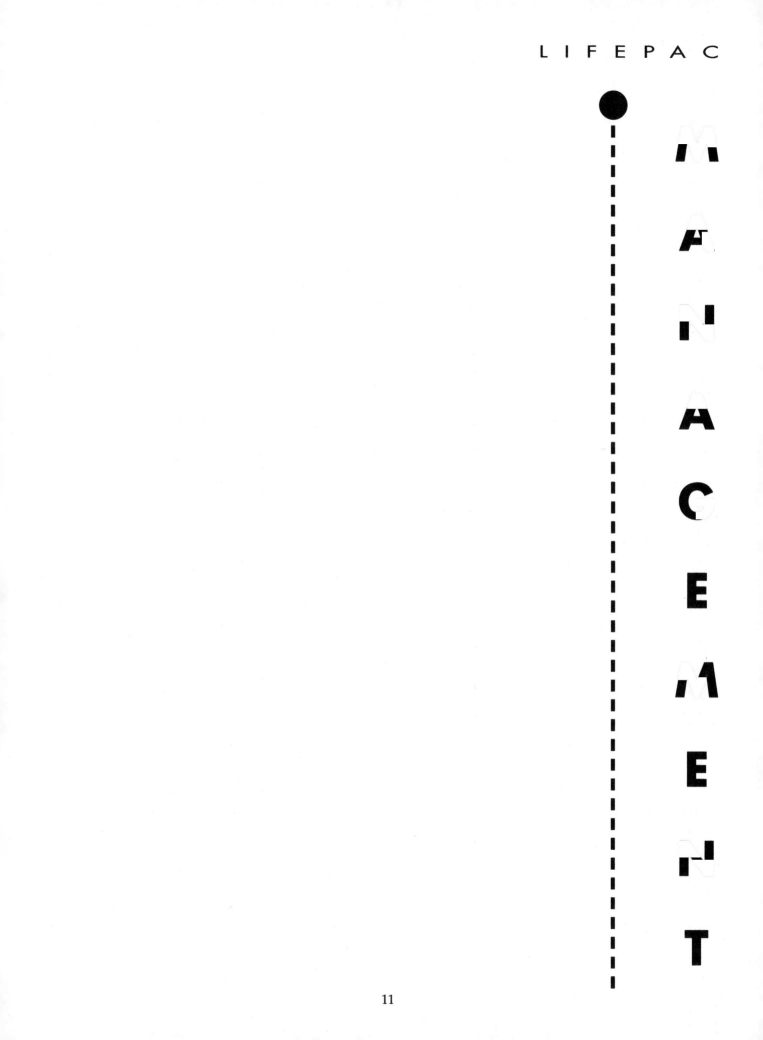

MANAGEMENT

STRUCTURE OF THE LIFEPAC CURRICULUM

The LIFEPAC curriculum is conveniently structured to provide one teacher handbook containing teacher support material with answer keys and ten student worktexts for each subject at grade levels two through twelve. The worktext format of the LIFEPACs allows the student to read the textual information and complete workbook activities all in the same booklet. The easy to follow LIFEPAC numbering system lists the grade as the first number(s) and the last two digits as the number of the series. For example, the Language Arts LIFEPAC at the 6th grade level, 5th book in the series would be LAN0605.

Each LIFEPAC is divided into 3 to 5 sections and begins with an introduction or overview of the booklet as well as a series of specific learning objectives to give a purpose to the study of the LIFEPAC. The introduction and objectives are followed by a vocabulary section which may be found at the beginning of each section at the lower levels, at the beginning of the LIFEPAC in the middle grades, or in the glossary at the high school level. Vocabulary words are used to develop word recognition and should not be confused with the spelling words introduced later in the LIFEPAC. The student should learn all vocabulary words before working the LIFEPAC sections to improve comprehension, retention, and reading skills.

Each activity or written assignment has a number for easy identification, such as 1.1. The first number corresponds to the LIFEPAC section and the number to the right of the decimal is the number of the activity.

Teacher checkpoints, which are essential to maintain quality learning, are found at various locations throughout the LIFEPAC. The teacher should check 1) neatness of work and penmanship, 2) quality of understanding (tested with a short oral quiz), 3) thoroughness of answers (complete sentences and paragraphs, correct spelling, etc.), 4) completion of activities (no blank spaces), and 5) accuracy of answers as compared to the answer key (all answers correct).

The self test questions are also number coded for easy reference. For example, 2.015 means that this is the 15th question in the self test of Section II. The first number corresponds to the LIFEPAC section, the zero indicates that it is a self test question, and the number to the right of the zero the question number.

The LIFEPAC test is packaged at the centerfold of each LIFEPAC. It should be removed and put aside before giving the booklet to the student for study.

Answer and test keys have the same numbering system as the LIFEPACs and appear at the back of this handbook. The student may be given access to the answer keys (not the test keys) under teacher supervision so that he can score his own work.

A thorough study of the Curriculum Overview by the teacher before instruction begins is essential to the success of the student. The teacher should become familiar with expected skill mastery and understand how these grade level skills fit into the overall skill development of the curriculum. The teacher should also preview the objectives that appear at the beginning of each LIFEPAC for additional preparation and planning.

TEST SCORING and GRADING

Answer keys and test keys give examples of correct answers. They convey the idea, but the student may use many ways to express a correct answer. The teacher should check for the essence of the answer, not for the exact wording. Many questions are high level and require thinking and creativity on the part of the student. Each answer should be scored based on whether or not the main idea written by the student matches the model example. "Any Order" or "Either Order" in a key indicates that no particular order is necessary to be correct.

Most self tests and LIFEPAC tests at the lower elementary levels are scored at 1 point per answer; however, the upper levels may have a point system awarding 2 to 5 points for various answers or questions. Further, the total test points will vary; they may not always equal 100 points. They may be 78, 85, 100, 105, etc.

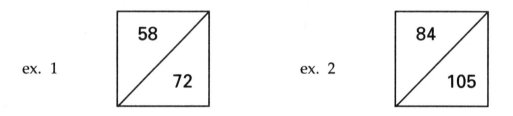

A score box similar to ex.1 above is located at the end of each self test and on the front of the LIFEPAC test. The bottom score, 72, represents the total number of points possible on the test. The upper score, 58, represents the number of points your student will need to receive an 80% or passing grade. If you wish to establish the exact percentage that your student has achieved, find the total points of his correct answers and divide it by the bottom number (in this case 72.) For example, if your student has a point total of 65, divide 65 by 72 for a grade of 90%. Referring to ex. 2, on a test with a total of 105 possible points, the student would have to receive a minimum of 84 correct points for an 80% or passing grade. If your student has received 93 points, simply divide the 93 by 105 for a percentage grade of 89%. Students who receive a score below 80% should review the LIFEPAC and retest using the appropriate Alternate Test found in the Teacher's Guide.

The following is a guideline to assign letter grades for completed LIFEPACs based on a maximum total score of 100 points.

LIFEPAC Test = 60% of the Total Score (or percent grade)
Self Test   = 25% of the Total Score (average percent of self tests)
Reports   = 10% or 10* points per LIFEPAC
Oral Work   = 5% or 5* points per LIFEPAC
*Determined by the teacher's subjective evaluation of the student's daily work.

Example:

LIFEPAC Test Score	=	92%	92 x .60	=	55 points
Self Test Average	=	90%	90 x .25	=	23 points
Reports				=	8 points
Oral Work				=	4 points

| TOTAL POINTS | | = | 90 points |

Grade Scale based on point system: 100 – 94 =   A

93 – 86	=	B
85 – 77	=	C
76 – 70	=	D
Below 70	=	F

TEACHER HINTS and STUDYING TECHNIQUES

LIFEPAC Activities are written to check the level of understanding of the preceding text. The student may look back to the text as necessary to complete these activities; however, a student should never attempt to do the activities without reading (studying) the text first. Self tests and LIFEPAC tests are never open book tests.

Language arts activities (skill integration) often appear within other subject curriculum. The purpose is to give the student an opportunity to test his skill mastery outside of the context in which it was presented.

Writing complete answers (paragraphs) to some questions is an integral part of the LIFEPAC Curriculum in all subjects. This builds communication and organization skills, increases understanding and retention of ideas, and helps enforce good penmanship. Complete sentences should be encouraged for this type of activity. Obviously, single words or phrases do not meet the intent of the activity, since multiple lines are given for the response.

Review is essential to student success. Time invested in review where review is suggested will be time saved in correcting errors later. Self tests, unlike the section activities, are closed book. This procedure helps to identify weaknesses before they become too great to overcome. Certain objectives from self tests are cumulative and test previous sections; therefore, good preparation for a self test must include all material studied up to that testing point.

The following procedure checklist has been found to be successful in developing good study habits in the LIFEPAC curriculum.

1. Read the introduction and Table of Contents.
2. Read the objectives.
3. Recite and study the entire vocabulary (glossary) list.
4. Study each section as follows:
    a. Read the introduction and study the section objectives.
    b. Read all the text for the entire section, but answer none of the activities.
    c. Return to the beginning of the section and memorize each vocabulary word and definition.
    d. Reread the section, complete the activities, check the answers with the answer key, correct all errors, and have the teacher check.
    e. Read the self test but do not answer the questions.
    f. Go to the beginning of the first section and reread the text and answers to the activities up to the self test you have not yet done.
    g. Answer the questions to the self test without looking back.
    h. Have the self test checked by the teacher.
    i. Correct the self test and have the teacher check the corrections.
    j. Repeat steps a–i for each section.

5. Use the SQ3R* method to prepare for the LIFEPAC test.
6. Take the LIFEPAC test as a closed book test.
7. LIFEPAC tests are administered and scored under direct teacher supervision. Students who receive scores below 80% should review the LIFEPAC using the SQ3R* study method and take the Alternate Test located in the Teacher Handbook. The final test grade may be the grade on the Alternate Test or an average of the grades from the original LIFEPAC test and the Alternate Test.

    *SQ3R: **S**can the whole LIFEPAC.

           Question yourself on the objectives.

           Read the whole LIFEPAC again.

           Recite through an oral examination.

           Review weak areas.

GOAL SETTING and SCHEDULES

Each school must develop its own schedule, because no single set of procedures will fit every situation. The following is an example of a daily schedule that includes the five LIFEPAC subjects as well as time slotted for special activities.

Possible Daily Schedule

8:15	–	8:25	Pledges, prayer, songs, devotions, etc.
8:25	–	9:10	Bible
9:10	–	9:55	Language Arts
9:55	–	10:15	Recess (juice break)
10:15	–	11:00	Mathematics
11:00	–	11:45	Social Studies
11:45	–	12:30	Lunch, recess, quiet time
12:30	–	1:15	Science
1:15	–		Drill, remedial work, enrichment*

*Enrichment: Computer time, physical education, field trips, fun reading, games and puzzles, family business, hobbies, resource persons, guests, crafts, creative work, electives, music appreciation, projects.

Basically, two factors need to be considered when assigning work to a student in the LIFEPAC curriculum.

The first is time. An average of 45 minutes should be devoted to each subject, each day. Remember, this is only an average. Because of extenuating circumstances a student may spend only 15 minutes on a subject one day and the next day spend 90 minutes on the same subject.

The second factor is the number of pages to be worked in each subject. A single LIFEPAC is designed to take 3 to 4 weeks to complete. Allowing about 3-4 days for LIFEPAC introduction, review, and tests, the student has approximately 15 days to complete the LIFEPAC pages. Simply take the number of pages in the LIFEPAC, divide it by 15 and you will have the number of pages that must be completed on a daily basis to keep the student on schedule. For example, a LIFEPAC containing 45 pages will require 3 completed pages per day. Again, this is only an average. While working a 45 page LIFEPAC, the student may complete only 1 page the first day if the text has a lot of activities or reports, but go on to complete 5 pages the next day.

Long range planning requires some organization. Because the traditional school year originates in the early fall of one year and continues to late spring of the following year, a calendar should be devised that covers this period of time. Approximate beginning and completion dates can be noted on the calendar as well as special occasions such as holidays, vacations and birthdays.

Since each LIFEPAC takes 3-4 weeks or eighteen days to complete, it should take about 180 school days to finish a set of ten LIFEPACs. Starting at the beginning school date, mark off eighteen school days on the calendar and that will become the targeted completion date for the first LIFEPAC. Continue marking the calendar until you have established dates for the remaining nine LIFEPACs making adjustments for previously noted holidays and vacations. If all five subjects are being used, the ten established target dates should be the same for the LIFEPACs in each subject.

FORMS

The sample weekly lesson plan and student grading sheet forms are included in this section as teacher support materials and may be duplicated at the convenience of the teacher.

The student grading sheet is provided for those who desire to follow the suggested guidelines for assignment of letter grades found on page 3 of this section. The student's self test scores should be posted as percentage grades. When the LIFEPAC is completed the teacher should average the self test grades, multiply the average by .25 and post the points in the box marked self test points. The LIFEPAC percentage grade should be multiplied by .60 and posted. Next, the teacher should award and post points for written reports and oral work. A report may be any type of written work assigned to the student whether it is a LIFEPAC or additional learning activity. Oral work includes the student's ability to respond orally to questions which may or may not be related to LIFEPAC activities or any type of oral report assigned by the teacher. The points may then be totaled and a final grade entered along with the date that the LIFEPAC was completed.

The Student Record Book which was specifically designed for use with the Alpha Omega curriculum provides space to record weekly progress for one student over a nine week period as well as a place to post self test and LIFEPAC scores. The Student Record Books are available through the current Alpha Omega catalog; however, unlike the enclosed forms these books are not for duplication and should be purchased in sets of four to cover a full academic year.

_____

_____

_____

_____

_____

_____

_____

_____

_____

_____

_____

_____

_____

_____

_____

_____

_____

_____

_____

_____

_____

_____

_____

_____

_____

_____

_____

_____

_____

WEEKLY LESSON PLANNER

Week of:

	Subject	Subject	Subject	Subject
Monday				
	Subject	Subject	Subject	Subject
Tuesday				
	Subject	Subject	Subject	Subject
Wednesday				
	Subject	Subject	Subject	Subject
Thursday				
	Subject	Subject	Subject	Subject
Friday				

WEEKLY LESSON PLANNER

Week of:

	Subject	Subject	Subject	Subject
Monday				
Tuesday	Subject	Subject	Subject	Subject
Wednesday	Subject	Subject	Subject	Subject
Thursday	Subject	Subject	Subject	Subject
Friday	Subject	Subject	Subject	Subject

Bible

LP #	Self Test Scores by Sections 1	2	3	4	5	Self Test Points	LIFEPAC Test	Oral Points	Report Points	Final Grade	Date
01											
02											
03											
04											
05											
06											
07											
08											
09											
10											

History & Geography

LP #	Self Test Scores by Sections 1	2	3	4	5	Self Test Points	LIFEPAC Test	Oral Points	Report Points	Final Grade	Date
01											
02											
03											
04											
05											
06											
07											
08											
09											
10											

Language Arts

LP #	Self Test Scores by Sections 1	2	3	4	5	Self Test Points	LIFEPAC Test	Oral Points	Report Points	Final Grade	Date
01											
02											
03											
04											
05											
06											
07											
08											
09											
10											

Student Name _____   Year _____

Mathematics

LP #	Self Test Scores by Sections 1	2	3	4	5	Self Test Points	LIFEPAC Test	Oral Points	Report Points	Final Grade	Date
01											
02											
03											
04											
05											
06											
07											
08											
09											
10											

Science

LP #	Self Test Scores by Sections 1	2	3	4	5	Self Test Points	LIFEPAC Test	Oral Points	Report Points	Final Grade	Date
01											
02											
03											
04											
05											
06											
07											
08											
09											
10											

Spelling/Electives

LP #	Self Test Scores by Sections 1	2	3	4	5	Self Test Points	LIFEPAC Test	Oral Points	Report Points	Final Grade	Date
01											
02											
03											
04											
05											
06											
07											
08											
09											
10											

TEACHER

**N
O
T
E
S**

INSTRUCTIONS FOR HISTORY & GEOGRAPHY

The LIFEPAC curriculum from grades two through twelve is structured so that the daily instructional material is written directly into the LIFEPACs. The student is encouraged to read and follow this instructional material in order to develop independent study habits. The teacher should introduce the LIFEPAC to the student, set a required completion schedule, complete teacher checks, be available for questions regarding both content and procedures, administer and grade tests, and develop additional learning activities as desired. Teachers working with several students may schedule their time so that students are assigned to a quiet work activity when it is necessary to spend instructional time with one particular student.

The Teacher Notes section of the Teacher's Guide lists the required or suggested materials for the LIFEPACs and provides additional learning activities for the students. The materials section refers only to LIFEPAC materials and does not include materials which may be needed for the additional activities. Additional learning activities provide a change from the daily school routine, encourage the student's interest in learning and may be used as a reward for good study habits.

Materials Needed for LIFEPAC

Required: Suggested:
                                                     atlas
                                                     world globe
                                                     encyclopedia

Additional Learning Activities

Section I   Quest and Conquest

1. Discuss these questions.
   a. What did Western Civilization get from Greece? from Rome? from Judaism? from Christianity?
   b. Why was Prince Henry's work so revolutionary?
   c. What kind of man was Columbus? a hero? an opportunist? a fool?
2. Do a class or individual project on spices to find out which were important, where they came from, and how they were used. Give a report.
3. Do research and a report or paper on the Viking exploration of America.
4. Different students should read about the lives of different *conquistadors*. Each should make a brief report to the class. Then, draw some conclusions. What kind of men were they?
5. Map out Magellan's trip around the world. Discuss what the circumstances would be like for the sailors at different points on the journey.
6. Discuss this question: Could the Aztec and Inca Empires have defeated the Spanish? If so, how?

Section II   The Chase

1. Discuss the circumstances in England that hindered exploration from there between 1490 and 1600.
2. Do research and a report or paper on the life of Francis Drake.
3. Do research and a report or paper on the Grand Banks.
4. Discuss what life would have been like on a ship exploring the New World in the late 1400s and early 1500s.
5. Create an ending for the story of Henry Hudson's life after he was marooned.
6. Discuss what drove the people of the 15th and 16th centuries to explore the earth, and compare it with why people might one day explore the stars.
7. Different students should read about the lives of Cartier, Champlain, Jolliet, Marquette, and LaSalle. Give a brief report to the class. Then, draw some conclusions. What kind of men were they?
8. Discuss the morality of the European custom of claiming for themselves any lands they "discovered."

Section III   The First Colonies

1. Each student or group of students should assume the role of a person in a Spanish colony—slave, Indian, mestizo, Spanish nobleman, etc. Discuss what your role is in society in the 1500s. Do the same for the French, Dutch, and English colonies.

2. Discuss how life was different in Spanish, Dutch, French, and English colonies and how it was the same.

3. Every student should write his own story about what happened to the Lost Colony. Read them in class. Discuss which is the most likely, the least likely, and the best story.

4. Discuss what life was like for the colonists in the early years of Jamestown.

5. Do some role playing and discuss or dramatize what it must have been like for Pocahontas to go to England.

6. Discuss the long-term effects of the three major events of 1619 at Jamestown. (The arrival of women and slaves, the founding of the House of Burgesses). Which was the most important event and why?

7. Discuss why the Indians would help the colonists and why they would fight them.

8. Discuss whether the Native Americans could have stopped European colonization of North America. If so, how?

Materials Needed for LIFEPAC

Required: Suggested:
                                 atlas
                                 globe
                                 encyclopedia

Additional Learning Activities

Section I   English Colonies

1. Do a special report on the founding and growth of one of the original thirteen colonies.
2. Find a sketch of the interior of the *Mayflower* and a description that lists its dimensions. Measure out how big it would be in an open field, marking its size with string or paint (if the teacher approves). Discuss what it would be like to live in that area with 100 other people, in unsanitary conditions for three months.
3. Discuss what conditions would be awful enough for you to leave your home to live in an undeveloped wilderness.
4. As a group, agree on a government for yourselves and try it out.
5. Discuss why the Massachusetts Bay Colony was so strict in religion.
6. Plan your own colony, including the government, religious laws, and citizenship requirements.
7. Read the Fundamental Orders of Connecticut and discuss it.
8. Do research and a report or paper about any one of the colonial founders.
9. Discuss which of the thirteen colonies you would prefer to live in and why.

Section II   Colonial Growth

1. Discuss why proprietary and company colonies failed to make a profit. How could they have been profitable?
2. Set up a mock colonial government and discuss one or more of these issues:
   a. The governor wants a larger salary.
   b. The assembly wants a judge removed from office.
   c. The citizens are worried about the threat of Indian attacks.
   d. A merchant with a monopoly (granted by the governor) on the sale of sugar to the colony has been charging very high prices.
   e. The governor has borrowed money from several important citizens to entertain the elite of the colony and cannot repay it.
   f. Farmers are letting their animals run loose in the capital city.
   g. The Board of Trade instructed the governor to improve the dock facilities at the main port of the colony.
   h. The English navy needs to set up a supply depot in the colony's main port.
3. Divide into three groups, each group assuming the role of colonists from one of the three sections of the English colonies. Defend your lifestyle in a debate.
4. Discuss the role of religion in the life of the colonists. How was it different from today? Are the changes good or bad?
5. Research and do a report or paper on Quakers, Puritans, or Deism.

6. Research the effects of the Great Awakening and discuss them in class.
7. Do research and a report or paper on Jonathan Edwards or George Whitefield.
8. Do research and a report or paper on the slave trade in the 1700s.

Section III   Wars with France

1. Do research and a report or paper on the European part of one of the wars discussed in this section.
2. Do research and a report or paper on the Iroquois Indians.
3. Discuss these questions:
   a. Why were France and Britain fighting at this time?
   b. Why were the Iroquois Indians so important in the American conflicts?
   c. Why did Edward Braddock act so stupidly?
   d. How did his experience in the French and Indian War help George Washington later in his life?
   e. How would the Revolution have been different if the Albany Plan had been accepted?
   f. What could have been done to foster the good will between the colonies and Britain after the French and Indian War to prevent the Revolution?
4. Do research and a report or paper on one of these people: William Pitt, Benjamin Franklin, Pontiac, James Wolfe, or the Marquis de Montcalm.
5. Make a model showing how Quebec was captured in the 1760s.
6. Divide into two groups, colonists and the British government, and debate the Proclamation of 1763.

Materials Needed for LIFEPAC

Required: Suggested:
                                            encyclopedia
                                            atlas

Additional Learning Activities

Section I   Growing Conflict

1. Discuss these questions with your class.
   a. Prior to the American Revolution, people lived quietly and submissively under oppressive governments. What changed this pattern in the New World?
   b. Can you single out one factor that put the colonists on a "collision course" with the British?
   c. Can you see the hand of God in the series of incidents that led to war and independence from Europe?
   d. Analyze one incident leading the British and the colonists to war; e.g., the Boston Massacre or the Intolerable Acts, etc. Could it have been resolved better, in a way that would have reconciled the two sides?
2. Act out a fireside chat between two colonial groups. The first group should argue that God requires us to obey the British government and honor the king. The other should argue that we have a God-given right to rebel. Use the Bible for reference. Engage in a spirited conversation.
3. Isolate one cause of the American Revolution, and do an in-depth research of the personalities involved. Emphasize their conviction and sincerity and the degree to which they appeared to be guided either by the spirit of the world or the Spirit which is from God.
4. Write a paper defending the British position that the colonists had a responsibility to alleviate the British war debts.
5. Assume you are the members of the Second Continental Congress and debate the Declaration of Independence. Which parts would you keep, and which would you change? Then, as a wealthy member of colonial society, decide if you would sign the document or not. (If you sign and the cause fails, you will hang for treason.)
6. Divide up a list of the lesser known men who signed the Declaration of Independence and have each person research one of them. Report to the class and draw some conclusions about what kind of men they were.

Section II   War

1. Debate this topic: "Resolved: The French, not the Americans, won the Revolutionary War."
2. Choose a battle in the Revolution and do a model or diagram of it.

3. Do a one- or two-page paper on any of these people: Thomas Paine, Benedict Arnold, Ethan Allen, George Rogers Clark, Nathanael Greene, Lafayette, Baron von Steuben, Horatio Gates, Daniel Morgan, John Paul Jones, Benjamin Lincoln, or Nathan Hale.
4. Discuss what you believe were the major mistakes made by the British.
5. Discuss what America would be like today if Washington had decided to make himself king. Research Napoleon and the French Revolution for ideas.

Section III   Constitution
1. Read a copy of the Articles of Confederation. (Check at your local library or on the Internet). Discuss what problems you find in it.
2. Discuss what the United States would be like today if the government did not allow territories to become states with equal rights.
3. Assemble some statistics on the men at the Constitutional Convention: their ages, wealth, backgrounds, experience in the Revolution, etc. Discuss the results.
4. Read and discuss all or parts of *The Federalist*.
5. Research one of these men, and report on what impact they had on the founding of the United States of America: Samuel Adams, John Adams, Thomas Jefferson, Benjamin Franklin, James Madison, Alexander Hamilton, John Marshall, or John Jay.
6. Read in class and discuss the Constitution of the United States. Possible topics include (but are not limited to):
   a. Why has it lasted so long?
   b. Why did the compromises work?
   c. Do the checks and balances still work today?
   d. How does the elector system work to choose the president and what are the problems with that system?
   e. How would the government be limited if it could only do exactly what the Constitution stated and nothing else?
7. Read the Bill of Rights and discuss:
   a. Why were these particular Amendments so important?
   b. Which do you consider to be the most important and why?

Materials Needed for LIFEPAC

Required: Suggested:
                                             encyclopedia
                                             atlas

Additional Learning Activities

Section I   The Federalist Era

1. Discuss these questions:
    a. Why was George Washington an obvious choice for the first president?
    b. Why was Alexander Hamilton's finance plan so controversial?
    c. Should political parties have been avoided?
    d. In what way was the Whiskey Rebellion like the revolt against the Stamp Act?
    e. Why was Washington's two term precedent important?
    f. Could the U.S. have done anything to stop impressment?
    g. Why was the first change of power in 1800 so important?
    h. Why did America avoid alliances after the Convention of 1800?
2. Research the French Revolution and discuss why Americans would or would not approve of it.
3. Debate this statement: "Resolved: John Adams was an excellent president."
4. Research the Alien and Sedition Acts. Write a one-page paper on why these were a dangerous precedent for American liberties.

Section II   Jeffersonian Democracy

1. Research and write a two-page paper on the Enlightenment describing how it agreed with or disagreed with Christianity.
2. The modern Democratic Party sometimes claims Thomas Jefferson as its founder. Discuss how its beliefs compare to those of Jefferson.
3. Discuss the importance of *Marbury v. Madison*. What would American government be like without judicial power to invalidate laws—especially in reference to abortion?
4. Read about the Lewis and Clark Expedition. Discuss what it would be like exploring such an unknown land.
5. Assume the roles of members of the Senate in 1807 (most senators would be Democratic-Republicans), debate the Embargo Act, and vote on it.
6. Assume the roles of members of the House of Representatives in 1812 (some will have to be War Hawks), debate the declaration of war with Britain, and vote.
7. Research the war by Tecumseh. Do a paper or report on why it started and why it was dangerous to the new American republic.
8. Discuss why the U.S. went to war with so little practical preparation.

Section III   War of 1812

1. Prepare a model or diagram of any of the battles of the war.
2. Research and do a report or paper on the *U.S.S. Constitution*.
3. Discuss why the Americans wanted to capture Canada and why the effort failed.
4. Research the Napoleonic Wars in Europe, and discuss why Britain was so desperate to defeat Napoleon.
5. Discuss what the long-term effects would have been in America if the United States had agreed to the harsh terms offered by the British in early 1814 before the victories at Baltimore and Plattsburg Bay.
6. Debate this statement: "Resolved: America won the War of 1812."
7. Prepare a map of the major hard-surface roads in 1820.
8. Assume the role of the House of Representatives in 1816, debate the American System, and vote on it. (Be sure that someone takes the role of Henry Clay).
9. Discuss what caused the "Era of Good Feelings."
10. Create a mock Supreme Court, and argue one of these cases after researching it:
    a. *Marbury v. Madison*
    b. *Fletcher v. Peck*
    c. *Culloch v. Maryland*
    d. *Dartmouth College v. Woodard*
    e. *Cohens v. Virginia*
    f. *Gibbons v. Ogden*
11. Research the Monroe Doctrine. Give a report or write a paper describing its impact on the Western Hemisphere.

Materials Needed for LIFEPAC

Required:

Suggested:
atlas
encyclopedia

Additional Learning Activities

Section I   Jacksonian Era

1. Do a two-page biography of one of these men: Henry Clay, John C. Calhoun, or Daniel Webster.
2. Assume the role of the Senate in 1820 (half would be from slave states, half from free; a few would be strong unionist and a few strongly anti-slavery), debate the Missouri Compromise and vote on it.
3. Debate this statement: "Resolved: Andrew Jackson was a poor president."
4. Discuss these questions:
   a. Would you vote for John Quincy Adams for president?
   b. Were tariffs good or bad for the nation?
   c. Was Andrew Jackson good or bad for the United States?
   d. Was the campaign of 1828 more or less civilized than the most recent presidential campaign?
5. Re-enact the Webster-Hayne Debate, and evaluate the arguments.
6. Research the National Bank issue under Andrew Jackson. List the arguments that could be made for and against the Bank.
7. Research the Trail of Tears. Do a report or write a paper about it.
8. Debate the issue of nullification.
9. Research and discuss the causes of Panics in early American history.

Section II   Manifest Destiny

1. Debate the morality of Manifest Destiny.
2. Research the conflict between Britain and the U.S. over Maine. Summarize it in one page.
3. Read the true story of one person who traveled the Oregon Trail.
4. Play a computer game that requires you to survive a trip down the Oregon Trail.
5. Read a book on the Texas Revolution or the life of one of its heroes: Stephen Austin, Davy Crockett, Sam Houston, Jim Bowie, or William Travis.
6. Build a model or diagram of the battle for the Alamo or San Jacinto.
7. Read a detailed description of one of the battles in the Mexican War.
8. Do a two page biography of one of these men: Santa Anna, Zachary Taylor, Winfield Scott, or John C. Frémont.
9. As a class or by yourself assemble a list of Civil War generals who served in the Mexican War. Include with each a brief statement of their rank and accomplishments in the earlier war.
10. Discuss the Mexican War from the Mexican point of view.
11. Read the true story of one person who was in the California Gold Rush.

Section III   Growth and Division

1. Research and do a report for the government of 1850 on conditions in the textile factories, recommending laws to protect the workers.
2. Do a one-page paper on the development and impact of one of these inventions: mechanical reaper, telegraph, cotton gin, steamboat, railroad engines, sewing machine, or spinning jenny.
3. Read a description of travel and transport on the Erie Canal.
4. Build a model of a canal barge.
5. Read about the Irish potato famine, and discuss what you would have done had you been one of the farmers hit by it.
6. Research and discuss the American traditions that came from Germany.
7. Do a paper on one of the following: camp meetings, Charles Finney, Francis Asbury, Joseph Smith, Mormonism, Brigham Young, the settlement of Utah, the Seneca Falls Convention, William Wilberforce, or the temperance movement in the 1800s.
8. Assume the role of the Senate in 1850 (don't forget Webster, Calhoun, and Clay), debate the Compromise of 1850 and vote on it. (Half the senators were from slave states and half were from free ones.)
9. Read a book about the Underground Railroad or a person who worked on it.
10. Research and debate the morality of Perry's treaty with Japan.
11. Read *Uncle Tom's Cabin*.
12. Discuss why things became so out of control in "Bleeding Kansas."

Materials Needed for LIFEPAC

Required:

Suggested:
encyclopedia
atlas

Additional Learning Activities

Section I   Increasing Disunion

1. Discuss the issues that divided the country prior to the Civil War and whether or not war could have been avoided.
2. Discuss the issue of slavery as viewed by the North and the South in 1860 and from your own point of view today.
3. Discuss the people's reactions to the Dred Scott decision, and explain your own reaction.
4. Two students pretend they are Lincoln and Douglas and debate the issues of 1860.
5. Write a report on John Brown's Raid, the election of 1860, the Dred Scott Decision, the Abolitionist movement, black soldiers in the Civil War, or Bleeding Kansas; and present it to the class.
6. Research and do a report or paper on any Civil War political or military leader, north or south.

Section II   Civil War

1. Do a model or diagram of any battle.
2. Find and read personal stories of men and women (mainly nurses and spies) who served in the war.
3. Construct models of the *Merrimac* and the *Monitor*. Demonstrate why they could not harm each other.
4. Rent and watch the movie *Gettysburg*. Discuss.
5. Do a dramatic reading of the Gettysburg Address.
6. Research and do a report or paper on medical science in the 1860s.
7. Read an account of Andersonville prison.
8. After some research, do a re-enactment of Lee's surrender at Appomattox Courthouse.
9. Read an account of the conspiracy organized by John Wilkes Booth to assassinate Lincoln and other government leaders, and report to the class.
10. Bring in artifacts, memorabilia, documents, clothing and pictures (check the Internet) from the Civil War.

Section III   Reconstruction

1. Assume the role of the Senate in 1865 (only Union representatives), and debate the issue of what to do with the conquered Confederacy.
2. Discuss the impeachment of Andrew Johnson and why it happened.
3. Read and discuss the 13th, 14th, and 15th Amendments. What were they intended to do and what did they actually accomplish?

4. Read different stories of life in the south during Reconstruction and discuss them in class.
5. Research and discuss the methods of the Ku Klux Klan and other redeemers. Discuss why they thought they were right and how God viewed their actions.
6. Draw a map of Alaska, marking the locations of its many resources.
7. Read about Ulysses S. Grant's life. Then, debate what kind of a man, general and president he was.
8. Read about Boss Tweed and Tammany Hall.
9. Research and do a report or paper on the election of 1876 or how the Civil War changed the South.
10. Read about Lucy Web Hayes and discuss the role of the First Lady.

Materials Needed for LIFEPAC

Required: Suggested:
encyclopedia
atlas

Additional Learning Activities

Section I   The Gilded Age

1. Discuss why this era was called the Gilded Age. Give specific examples and then choose an alternate name for the era.
2. Research and do a report or paper on the transcontinental railroad, the Homestead Act, Andrew Carnegie, John D. Rockefeller, J.P. Morgan, Immigration in the late 1800s, the Knights of Labor, the American Federation of Labor, High Society life in the late 1800s, the Grange, or Thomas Edison.
3. Choose the topic of either "Immigration to the U.S." or "Homesteading on the Great Plains." Different students should read the personal stories of people who emigrated or homesteaded. Tell the person's story to the class and discuss him or her.
4. Debate this topic: "Resolved: Social Darwinism is an unavoidable result if you believe in evolution."
5. Make a collage of pictures contrasting how the wealthy and the poor lived in the Gilded Age.
6. As a class make a visual history of the circus in America.
7. Research and do a paper on one of the Indian nations of the Great Plains.
8. Do a diagram or model of the Battle of Little Big Horn. Discuss the mistakes made by Custer.
9. Read about how cowboys lived in the late 1800s. Rent and see a cowboy movie about a cattle drive. Write a short paper on how realistic the movie was, giving specific examples.
10. Discuss what it meant to the United States to no longer have a frontier.

Section II   Gilded Politics

1. Research and do a paper or report on James Blaine, Roscoe Conkling, Chester A. Arthur, Grover Cleveland, William McKinley, William Jennings Bryan, Theodore Roosevelt, or George Dewey.
2. Discuss why civil service reform finally passed.
3. Do some research on the subject and discuss why silver coinage was such a hot issue.
4. Debate this topic: "Resolved: American business owned the American government in the late 1800s before the Progressive reforms."
5. Discuss and decide who was the least notable president between 1880 and 1900.
6. Discuss whether or not the U.S. had any good reason to get into the Spanish-American War.
7. Read "yellow journalism" articles about Cuba and the Spanish-American War. Discuss them as journalism and propaganda. How do they compare to modern articles about sensational stories?

8. Research and do a report or paper on the annexation of Hawaii.
9. Read a book on the Spanish-American War.
10. Make a model or diagram of the capture of Santiago.
11. Assume the role of the House of Representatives in 1898, debate what to do with the islands ceded by Spain and vote on it.
12. Debate this issue: "Resolved: America became an imperialist nation after 1898."

Section III   The Progressive Era

1. Read a biography of any of the Progressive reformers or a book about their work.
2. Discuss why reform was so badly needed in the U.S.
3. Read a muckraking book or article from this era. Discuss it in class.
4. Discuss the Roosevelt Administration. Why was T.R. so popular and what did he actually accomplish?
5. Make a model or diagram of the Panama Canal.
6. Read about the Panama Canal and discuss whether or not the U.S. dealt fairly with the people of that nation.
7. Debate this issue: "Resolved: Theodore Roosevelt was an arrogant bully."
8. Discuss these questions:
    a. Why was it so difficult for William Taft to be president after Theodore Roosevelt?
    b. Why was Dollar Diplomacy such a bad idea?
    c. Was Taft really a Progressive?
    d. Why was the Model T so successful?
    e. Why was Woodrow Wilson such an unusual president?
    f. What mistakes did Wilson make in regard to Mexico?
9. Build a model of the Wright Brother's airplane.
10. Write a paper or work as a class to speculate how America would be different if the Progressive reformers had failed.

Materials Needed for LIFEPAC

Required:

Suggested:
atlas
encyclopedia

Additional Learning Activities

Section I   World War I

1. Discuss whether or not the U.S. could have or should have stayed out of World War I.
2. Build a model of a World War I trench system
3. Read about conditions on a World War I U-boat.
4. In class or on paper give the German point of view on the U-boat issue.
5. Bring in memorabilia, artifacts, documents, clothing and pictures (check the internet) from World War I.
6. Read about the Russian Revolution and discuss why it happened.
7. Discuss why the Treaty of Versailles was a failure and what (if anything) could have been done to save it.
8. Research and do a report or paper on one of these topics: weapons of World War I; World War I from a German, French or British point of view; the League of Nations; or the influenza pandemic of 1918-19.
9. Rent and see the movie *Sergeant York,* starring Gary Cooper. Discuss in class.
10. Read personal accounts of soldiers in World War I and discuss them.

Section II   The Great Depression

1. Discuss how the "Roaring Twenties" are like and unlike society today.
2. Read a biography of Warren Harding, Calvin Coolidge, Herbert Hoover, Al Capone, Charles Lindbergh, Babe Ruth, or Franklin D. Roosevelt.
3. Collect personal accounts of life in the Great Depression from older members of your family or people you know. Present them in class.
4. Research and do a report or paper on one of these topics: the Scopes Monkey Trial, the Fundamentalists, flappers, Prohibition, the birth of the American auto industry, the Stock Market Crash of 1929, the activities of Ku Klux Klan in the 1920s, the kidnapping of Charles Lindbergh's son, and any one or more of the New Deal organizations.
5. Research the basic facts of either the Sacco and Vanzetti trial or the Scopes Monkey Trial. Present the trial in class, complete with attorneys, judge, and jury.
6. Have a person who lived during the Great Depression speak to your class. Prepare questions in advance.
7. Research and report on the scandals of the Harding Administration.
8. Have a debate on this issue: "Resolved: Prohibition was good for the nation."
9. Research the treatment of black Americans as soldiers during World War I and in the 1920s.
10. Research and report or do a paper on conditions in Germany between the World Wars.

Section III   World War II

1. Read a biography of one of these people: Adolf Hitler, Benito Mussolini, Joseph Stalin, Winston Churchill, Bernard Montgomery, Edwin Rommel, Charles de Gaulle, George Marshall, Dwight Eisenhower, George Patton, Omar Bradley, Douglas MacArthur, or Chester Nimitz.
2. Bring in artifacts, memorabilia, documents, clothing, and pictures (check the internet) from World War II.
3. Research the history of your family in World War II (everyone was affected by the war in some way). Do a paper or report on the results.
4. Rent and watch a movie about a specific incident or battle in World War II, like Iwo Jima or D-day. Read about the incident and discuss how realistic the movie was.
5. Discuss these questions:
   a. Would the U.S. have gotten into World War II without Pearl Harbor?
   b. Could the Allies have won without the United States?
   c. What would the world be like today if Hitler and the Japanese had been victorious?
   d. How did the war change America?
   e. Was the atomic bomb a moral weapon to use in battle?
6. Draw a diagram or make a model of any World War II battle.
7. Have a World War II veteran speak to your class. Prepare questions in advance.
8. (Teachers should use some caution on this assignment and consider previewing any reading assigned to the students). Read about Nazi and Japanese atrocities. Discuss what these incidents tell us about human nature.
9. As a class, put together a Holocaust memorial using pictures, facts, and brief stories from survivors.
10. Debate one of these topics:
   a. "Resolved: Doolittle's Raid was an American victory."
   b. "Resolved: The Invasion of North Africa unnecessarily delayed the attack on Hitler's Europe."
   c. "Resolved: The Japanese military culture made the atomic bomb unavoidable."
11. Rent and watch a documentary on any aspect of World War II that interests you.
12. Make a collage of the damage caused by World War II in Europe.
13. Do a dramatic reading of one of Winston Churchill's wartime speeches.
14. Research and report or do a paper on the effects of the atomic bomb on Hiroshima and Nagasaki.

Materials Needed for LIFEPAC

Required:

Suggested:
atlas
encyclopedia

Additional Learning Activities

Section I   Hot or Cold?

1. Discuss these questions:
   a. Was containment a good policy?
   b. Who was right about how to proceed in the Korean War: Eisenhower or MacArthur?
   c. Why did the U.S. get so involved in Vietnam?
   d. Why was communism so frightening to Americans?
   e. Could the West have stopped the Berlin Wall from being built?
   f. Should America have tried to prevent the communist takeover of China?
   g. What would have happened after World War II if America had returned to its traditional isolation from foreign problems?
   h. Why didn't the Cold War ever become hot?
2. Research and do a report or paper on one of these topics: the Korean War, the Berlin Airlift, the Marshall Plan, NATO, the U-2 Affair, the Space Race, the Cuban Missile Crisis, the Bay of Pigs, the Berlin Wall, the Gulf of Tonkin Resolution, or the Anti-war protests of the 1960s and 70s.
3. Read personal accounts of soldiers in the Korean or Vietnam War and discuss them in class.
4. Invite a Korean or Vietnamese War veteran to speak to your class about the war and the public reaction to it. Prepare questions in advance.
5. Bring in memorabilia, artifacts, documents, clothing, and pictures (check the internet) from the Korean or Vietnam Wars.
6. Read about life under communism in eastern Europe and discuss it in class.
7. Talk to someone who was old enough to remember Kennedy's assassination. Ask about their reaction and memories of the investigation afterward.
8. Read about the Hungarian revolt in 1956 or the one in Czechoslovakia in 1968.
9. Watch a documentary on the Korean or Vietnam War.
10. Assume the role of the Senate in 1964 (two-thirds of the people should be Democrats and one-third Republicans), debate the Gulf of Tonkin Resolution and vote on it.
11. Invite someone who participated in the anti-war protests to talk to your class. Prepare questions for them in advance.

Section II   Between War and Watergate

1. Read a biography of one of these people: Harry Truman, John Kennedy, Lyndon B. Johnson, Richard Nixon, Joseph McCarthy, W.E.B. DuBois, Booker T. Washington, Martin Luther King, Jr., Robert Kennedy, Alger Hiss, or George McGovern.
2. Discuss why the Civil Rights Movement succeeded.

3. Research the facts in the Alger Hiss perjury trial or the trial of the Rosenburgs. Try one of the cases with your own attorneys, judge, and jury.
4. Research and create a chart showing the progress of the Watergate scandal.
5. Knowing that the police in Birmingham, Alabama were likely to attack civil rights protesters, write a one-page paper explaining why you would or would not have joined a march through that city in 1963.
6. Do a dramatic reading of Martin Luther King's speech "I Have a Dream."
7. Assume the role of the U.S. Senate in 1974 (Democrats controlled slightly more than half of the seats, 56 to 42 with 2 independents), debate and vote on the impeachment of Richard Nixon.
8. Research and do a report or paper on one of these topics: the U.S. effort to land on the moon, Hippies, Abortion in America, Busing in the 1970s, Détente, Black education under "Separate but Equal" (before 1954), Divorce in America, The election of 1948 (Truman v. Dewey), the hunt for communists in the 1950s, or the Peace Corps.
9. Do a class project to assemble a presentation on the Civil Rights Movement, using pictures and personal stories.
10. Pretend you are a journalist with Nixon in China in 1972. Do some research and write a one-page paper describing the visit and explaining its importance to your readers in the United States.

Section III   Unexpected Victory
1. Write a two-page biography on one of these people: Gerald Ford, Jimmy Carter, Anwar Sadat, Menachem Begin, Ayatollah Khomeini, Ronald Reagan, George Bush, Mikhail Gorbachev, Norman Schwarzkopf, Colin Powell, Saddam Hussein, or Boris Yeltsin.
2. Discuss these questions:
   a. Should Gerald Ford have pardoned Richard Nixon?
   b. Could the Iran Hostage Crisis have been resolved quickly?
   c. Does the U.S. still have an energy crisis?
   d. Should the U.S. have interfered in Nicaragua, Grenada, or Panama?
   e. Is the world safer or more dangerous after the fall of communism?
3. Research the fall of communism in one nation in Eastern Europe. Report to the class.
4. Ask a Persian Gulf War veteran to speak to your class. Prepare questions in advance.
5. Survey your parents, teachers, and adult friends about the fall of communism. Did they expect it to happen? What did it mean to them?
6. Read about the Persian Gulf War and the occupation of Kuwait.
7. Compare a 1988 map of Europe with a 1998 map. What is different?
8. Research and do a report or paper on one of the nations of Eastern Europe or the former Soviet Union after the fall of communism.
9. Research and prepare a chart showing the development of the Iran-Contra Scandal.

Materials Needed for LIFEPAC

Required: Suggested:
                                   encyclopedia
                                   atlas

Additional Learning Activities

Section I   Recent America

1. Research and do a report or paper on one of these topics: NAFTA, the 1992 rescue mission in Somalia, the Tiananmen Square rebellion and massacre, contract with America with its results, Yugoslavia since the fall of communism, computers, medical technology, or the impeachment of William Clinton.
2. Research and discuss in class, U.S. relations with China, Cuba, or North Korea in the last year.
3. Make a chart of the U.S. national debt for as far back as you can find.
4. Research and discuss this question: Did the U.S. interference in Haiti in 1994 help that nation?
5. Do a two-page paper on the benefits and problems of the Internet.
6. Choose a Christian organization that is fighting the decline in American morals. Do research and assemble a list of what they are doing. Discuss in class whether you believe their efforts will be effective or not.

Section II and III   Reviews

1. Discuss how the founding fathers interpreted the Constitution, and compare it with the politicians and judges of today.
2. Do a paper or report comparing life in Virginia (or any other colony/state) in 1650, 1750, 1820, 1880, and 1950.
3. Do a paper or report comparing life in any western state at the time it was first settled, at statehood, during the Great Depression, and in the 1960s.
4. In a class discussion or in a paper, compare and contrast the impeachments of Johnson and Clinton.
5. Assemble a display that shows the battle uniforms of the U.S. army from the Revolution until the Persian Gulf War.
6. Research and do a report, paper, or display that shows how firearms and artillery used by the U.S. armed forces have changed from the Revolution to the Persian Gulf War.
7. Assemble a display that shows changes in the architecture of American homes from 1607 to 2000.
8. Invite a Native American to speak to your class about American history from his people's point of view. Prepare questions in advance.
9. Debate this topic: "Resolved: The Monroe Doctrine is still an important part of American policy."
10. Make a wall map for your classroom showing the outline of the growth of the United States (show the Louisiana Purchase, Mexican Cession and so forth), marking each state with the date it was admitted to the Union.

11. Prepare a wall display for your classroom of the presidents of the United States. Include a picture, dates in office, and a brief list of his accomplishments.

12. Rank the presidents of the United States from best to worst, in your opinion.

13. Write a two-page paper on the subject "The most important event in American history was… " describing and defending your choice.

14. Class project: Describe a journey between two cities that were important to your region at different times in American History. Each student should be assigned a different point in time. Share your reports with the class. (For example: If you are in New York, you might pick a trip between Buffalo and New York City in 1700, 1800, 1830, 1880, 1920, 1950, and 1990. If you are in Missouri, you might pick a trip from St. Louis to any of the major pioneer destinations or to New Orleans. Use your imagination!!)

15. Do a history of your city or town as a part of American History.

16. Research and do a report or paper comparing Christian worship in your church today with worship in America's history (go back at least 100 years).

17. Discuss how Democrats Andrew Jackson, Grover Cleveland, Harry Truman, and William Clinton would have gotten along together in politics.

18. Discuss how Republicans Abraham Lincoln, Benjamin Harrison, Theodore Roosevelt, and Ronald Reagan would have gotten along together in politics.

19. Discuss these questions:

    a. What was the biggest change in American life from 1776 to 1880? from 1880 to 2000?

    b. What was the biggest change in American government from 1776 to 1880? from 1880 to 2000?

    c. What would most Americans have thought about their homeland in 1750? in 1815? in 1860? in 1890? in 1916? in 1935? in 1945? in 1960? (Teachers, this is a good question to use for review because the students have to know what is happening on those dates to answer.)

    d. What made the United States the most powerful nation on earth?

    e. What is your favorite part of American history and why?

A L T E R N A T E

T E S T S

Reproducible Tests
for use with the History &
Geography 800 Teacher's
Guide

Name _____

Match these people with the best description of the land they explored. Some answers will be used more than once (each answer, 2 points).

1. _____ Marquette
2. _____ La Salle
3. _____ Columbus
4. _____ Balboa
5. _____ Magellan
6. _____ Drake
7. _____ Coronado
8. _____ Cartier
9. _____ Ponce de León
10. _____ Champlain
11. _____ De Soto
12. _____ Hudson
13. _____ Cabot
14. _____ Jolliet
15. _____ Ericson

a. the Mississippi River
b. Florida
c. the Caribbean, Central America, and northern South America
d. New York and northern Canada
e. Newfoundland
f. St. Lawrence River
g. Isthmus of Panama
h. coast of South America and the Pacific Ocean on the way to Asia
i. west coast of North America on the way to Asia
j. southwestern United States
k. Mississippi River, Georgia, Alabama, Mississippi, and Arkansas
l. St. Lawrence, Great Lakes, east coast south to Massachusetts
m. Ohio River valley, Mississippi River

Name the European country that sponsored each item or person (each answer, 2 points).

16. _____ Jamestown
17. _____ Columbus
18. _____ opening the trade route around Africa
19. _____ claimed the Mississippi River basin by 1700
20. _____ Fort Orange, settlements on the Hudson River
21. _____ the first permanent European settlement in the United States
22. _____ Cortes and Pizarro
23. _____ Magellan
24. _____ persecuted Huguenots, encouraged *coureurs de bois*
25. _____ Detroit, New Orleans, Quebec
26. _____ Roanoke, John Cabot

27. _____ claimed Florida and southwestern U.S. by 1700

28. _____ claimed the U.S. east coast and Hudson Bay area by 1700

29. _____ divided up the non-Catholic world with Portugal with the Treaty of Tordesillas

30. _____ few settlers, mostly fur traders, no religious or political freedom, best relations with the Indians

31. _____ House of Burgesses, Elizabeth I, James I

32. _____ Isabela, Santa Fe, San Diego

33. _____ Champlain, Cartier

34. _____ Invincible Armada, a tremendous wealth of gold and silver from Mexico and Peru

35. _____ West India Company, purchased Manhattan Island, *patroon* system

Identify each of the following items or persons (each answer, 3 points).

36. _____ Traveled to China in the 1200s, wrote a book that interested Europe in the Far East

37. _____ Two hundred year attempt to take the Holy Land from the Muslims, brought Europe into contact with Asian markets and science

38. _____ Cash crop of Virginia

39. _____ The four cultural ancestors of Western Civilization

_____

_____

_____

40. _____ settlement established by the London Company of Virginia in 1607 on a marshy peninsula

41. _____ the continent the very first American settlers came from

42. _____ prince who organized voyages around Africa to Asia

Date _____

Score _____

Name _____

Name the colony associated with each item or person (each answer, 3 points).

1. _____ William Penn, received for a debt Charles II owed Penn's father

2. _____ Roger Williams

3. _____ founded by the Dutch West India Company

4. _____ first of the thirteen colonies

5. _____ had largest port city in the colonies at the Revolution

6. _____ Catholic haven

7. _____ The Fundamental Orders were the first constitution

8. _____ Pennsylvania's outlet to the sea

9. _____ Lord Baltimore

10. _____ James Oglethorpe

11. _____ settled by poor farmers from Virginia, lacked good ports

12. _____ Puritan colony, took its charter to America

13. _____ haven for debtors, buffer against Spanish America

14. _____ order of ownership: Duke of York, Berkeley and Careret, Quakers, royal

15. _____ group of eight wealthy proprietors founded it, settled from the West Indies, established an aristocratic, slave holding economy

Choose the correct conflict for each item. Some are used more than once (each answer, 3 points).

King William's War	Queen Anne's War	King Philip's War
King George's War	Pontiac's War	Bacon's Rebellion
French and Indian War	Glorious Revolution	

16. _____ The one British-French conflict that brought numbers of British troops to the colonies.

17. _____ Largest Indian War of the colonial period.

18. _____ James II left England, William and Mary became the rulers

19. _____ War of the Grand Alliance, or League of Augsburg, in Europe

20. _____ led by a popular western Virginia landowner against the governor

21. _____ Matacom, leader of the Wampanoag, tried to drive out the New England settlers

22. _____ cost the French almost all of their land in North America

23. _____ War of the Spanish Succession in Europe

24. _____ General Braddock ambushed and killed on the way to Fort Dusquesne

25. _____ Indians attacked all along the British frontier, first at the forts

26. _____ War of the Austrian Succession in Europe, colonists captured Louisbourg

27. _____ Washington gained his military experience and reputation

Name each one (each answer, 3 points).

28. The American revival of the 1730s and 40s: _____

29. Plymouth colonists' agreement to form a government: _____

_____

30. The union of New York, New England, and New Jersey created by James II:

_____

31. The three parts of most colonial governments:

a. _____

b. _____

c. _____

32. Decree that ordered the colonists not to settle west of the Appalachians:

_____

80 / 100

Date _____
Score _____

Name _____

Match these names (each answer, 2 points).

1.	____ French admiral	a. Washington
2.	____ turning point of the war	b. Jefferson
3.	____ president, Second Continental Congress	c. Lafayette
4.	____ Act that closed Boston harbor	d. Cornwallis
5.	____ German mercenaries	e. Yorktown
6.	____ author of *Common Sense*	f. Saratoga
7.	____ plan at Constitutional Convention to base representation on population	g. Paine
8.	____ final major battle of the war	h. Adams
9.	____ American general who lost at Guilford Courthouse and Eutaw Springs but freed most of the south	i. Townshend
10.	____ Acts that restricted American trade	j. Greene
11.	____ surprise attack day after Christmas 1776, revived the American cause	k. Trenton
12.	____ author of Declaration of Independence	l. Rochambeau
13.	____ French aristocrat, volunteer American officer	m. de Grasse
14.	____ hero of Saratoga and Ticonderoga, traitor	n. Hancock
15.	____ Acts taxing tea, lead, glass and other British goods	o. Arnold
16.	____ American commander at Yorktown	p. Burgoyne
17.	____ Boston radical, Committees of Correspondence	q. Virginia
18.	____ French army commander at Yorktown	r. Navigation
19.	____ British commander at Saratoga	s. Intolerable
20.	____ British commander at Yorktown	t. Hessians

Complete the following (each answer, 3 points).

21. What were the three reactions in America to the Stamp Act?

    a. _____

    b. _____

    c. _____

22. The American army spent the winter of 1777-78 drilling under harsh conditions at _____ near Philadelphia.

23.   The Americans gained a valuable alliance in 1778. What nation was it and who was the
        American representative there?

        a. _____

        b. _____

24.   The Intolerable Acts were a British reaction to what event?

        _____

25.   What two English liberties were the American colonists denied in Admiralty Court?

        a. _____

        b. _____

26.   Name the petition sent by the Second Continental Congress in 1775 asking the king to
        intervene on behalf of the colonies and avert further hostilities.

        _____

27.   Why was Britain so in need of money after 1763?

        _____

28.   Name two things that the Constitutional Convention delegates compromised about.

        a. _____

        b. _____

29.   What was the first constitution for the United States?

        _____

30.   Name the famous series of essays written in support of the Constitution by Madison,
        Hamilton, and Jay. _____

31.   Name two advantages the Americans had in the Revolutionary War.

        a. _____

        b. _____

32.   What were the three branches of government set up by the Constitution?

        a. _____

        b. _____

        c. _____

80 / 100

Date _____

Score _____

Name _____

Match the following (each answer, 2 points).

1. _____ XYZ Affair

2. _____ War Hawks

3. _____ Whiskey Rebellion

4. _____ Federalist

5. _____ Democratic-Republican

6. _____ Alien and Sedition Acts

7. _____ Convention of 1800

8. _____ Citizen Genêt

9. _____ Battle of New Orleans

10. _____ Battle of Plattsburg Bay

11. _____ Barbary pirates

12. _____ *Chesapeake-Leopard* Affair

13. _____ *U.S.S. Constitution*

14. _____ Louisiana Purchase

15. _____ Lewis and Clark

16. _____ Tecumseh

17. _____ *Marbury v. Madison*

18. _____ Embargo Act

19. _____ Jay's Treaty

20. _____ War of 1812

21. _____ Battle of Lake Erie

22. _____ Spain ceded Florida

23. _____ American System

24. _____ Nationalism

25. _____ Monroe Doctrine

a. French envoy who threatened U.S. neutrality by trying to get Americans into British-French war

b. after Andrew Jackson defeated the Seminoles

c. Henry Clay's proposal to use higher tariffs to aid transportation in the states

d. the nation's reaction after the War of 1812

e. Europe told to stay out of America

f. *Old Ironsides*, famous U.S. frigate

g. French try to get bribes to negotiate

h. political party of John Adams

i. revolt against the excise tax

j. land bought from France west of Mississippi

k. expedition that explored Louisiana Territory

l. American victory after war ended

m. Jefferson sent the navy against them

n. victory by Oliver Perry, "We have met the enemy and they are ours."

o. organized Indian confederacy against U.S.

p. young congressmen from the west who wanted war with Britain

q. American-British agreement under Washington that held off war, but was very unpopular

r. Jefferson's attempt to avoid war by stopping trade

s. stopped the British from invading New York along Lake Champlain

t. political party that dominated early 1800s

u. Supreme Court claimed for itself the right to declare laws unconstitutional

v. British warship fires on American ship, seizes four seamen

w. French-American agreement that ended the Revolutionary alliance

x. Federalist laws to silence opposition

y. Second War for Independence

Name the person (each answer, 3 points).

26. _____ Third president, first secretary of state

27. _____ Only president to receive unanimous electoral vote

28. _____ President of the "Era of Good Feelings"

29. _____ First secretary of treasury, set the nation's finances up securely

30. _____ Vice president under Jefferson, tried to start a conspiracy in the west, acquitted of treason

31. _____ Federalist Chief Justice of the Supreme Court, set up the court's power

32. _____ American general who defeated the Creek Indians and the British at New Orleans

33. _____ Vice president under Washington, second president

34. _____ Speaker of the House, leader of War Hawks

35. _____ American victor at Tippecanoe and the Thames

Write *true* **or** *false* **in the blank** (each answer, 1 point).

36. _____ One result of the War of 1812 was the beginning of manufacturing tradition in America.

37. _____ One result of the War of 1812 was the end of wars with Britain.

38. _____ One result of the War of 1812 was the end of the Democratic-Republican party.

39. _____ The Great Seal of the United States has an eagle on one side and the White House on the other.

40. _____ The southern states agreed to allow the Revolutionary war debts to be taken by the federal government in exchange for the capital being located in the south.

41. _____ Jefferson believed in "strict construction" of the Constitution and lived by that when he was in office.

42. _____ The lack of a national bank helped the nation during the War of 1812.

43. _____ The Federalist party left only a legacy of disunity and factionalism.

44. _____ Washington urged the nation to avoid permanent alliances in his *Farewell Address* and the nation followed that advice for years.

45. _____ The British were supporting the Indians harassing the American frontier before the War of 1812.

46. _____ Jefferson reduced the national debt and ran the government as cheaply as possible.

47. _____ The election of 1800 was important because it was the first peaceful change of political power from one party to another.

48. _____ British impressment of sailors on American ships was an issue under every president from Washington to Madison.

49. _____ John Adams lost his popularity because he refused to go to war with France.

50. _____ New Englanders heavily supported the War of 1812.

51. _____ George Washington served one term as president.

52. _____ John Adams and his vice president were from different parties.

53. _____ The Hartford Convention destroyed what was left of the popularity of the early Democratic Party.

54. _____ Tecumseh was killed at the Battle of Tippecanoe.

55. _____ America had an excellent, well-supplied navy and army ready by the time the War of 1812 started.

Date _____

Score _____

Name _____

Match these people (each answer, 2 points).

1.	_____ telegraph	a.	Henry Clay
2.	_____ "His Accidency," Whig with Democrat ideas	b.	Andrew Jackson
3.	_____ hero of northern Mexico campaign and later president	c.	Robert Fulton
4.	_____ Compromise of 1850 was the only major accomplishment of his accidental presidency	d.	James K. Polk
5.	_____ added more land to the U.S. than any other president, first "dark horse" candidate	e.	John Quincy Adams
6.	_____ sewing machine	f.	John Calhoun
7.	_____ mechanical reaper	g.	Martin Van Buren
8.	_____ hero of Mexico City	h.	John Tyler
9.	_____ pro-south northern president, wanted to add Cuba to the U.S., embarrassed by the Osten Manifesto	i.	Elias Howe
10.	_____ hero of Tippecanoe, shortest presidency in U.S. history	j.	Eli Whitney
11.	_____ steamboat	k.	Franklin Pierce
12.	_____ fought against the National Bank and for Peggy Eaton as president	l.	Daniel Webster
13.	_____ the Great Compromiser, leader in Congress, never became president	m.	Sam Houston
14.	_____ opened the first machine operated textile factory in America	n.	Zachary Taylor
15.	_____ hand-chosen successor to Andrew Jackson, inherited the Panic of 1837	o.	Cyrus McCormick
16.	_____ leader of the south, favored nullification	p.	Samuel Slater
17.	_____ leader of the Texas Revolution, victor at San Jacinto	q.	Winfield Scott
18.	_____ interchangeable parts, cotton gin	r.	Samuel F. B. Morse
19.	_____ served with distinction as a representative in the House after being president, "Old Man Eloquent"	s.	Millard Fillmore
20.	_____ northern orator, famous for debate with Haynes "Liberty and Union, now and forever, one and inseparable."	t.	William H. Harrison

Match these items (each item, 2 points).

21. _____ the removal of the Indians of the southeast to land across the Mississippi

22. _____ secretive, anti-immigrant group

23. _____ California admitted as a free state, popular sovereignty in the Mexican Cession

24. _____ Polk's way of getting California

25. _____ revival

26. _____ popular anti-slavery novel

27. _____ the first workable steamboat

28. _____ attempt by South Carolina to void enforcement of the tariff in their state

29. _____ Treaty that ended the Mexican War and gave the U.S. the Mexican Cession

30. _____ punished people who aided runaway slaves and turned many northerners against slavery

31. _____ replaced canals as the major carriers of bulk cargo in the U.S.

32. _____ religion started by Joseph Smith, practiced polygamy

33. _____ change from farming and hand crafts to industry and machines

34. _____ "Fifty-four Forty or Fight," never happened, British and U.S. agreed to extend the 49th parallel as the boundary

35. _____ Maine admitted as a free state, no slavery north of 36° 30' in Louisiana Territory

36. _____ bought from Mexico for a southern railroad to California

37. _____ prevented any petition on slavery from being presented in Congress, John Quincy Adams successfully fought it

38. _____ a group that helped runaway slaves safely reach Canada

39. _____ early locomotive that lost a race with a horse

40. _____ America should expand all over the continent

a. Nullification Crisis

b. Missouri Compromise

c. Mexican War

d. Gag Rule

e. "Trail of Tears"

f. Industrial Revolution

g. Manifest Destiny

h. Gadsden Purchase

i. Oregon

j. Guadalupe Hidalgo

k. *Tom Thumb*

l. *Clermont*

m. Know-Nothing Party

n. Second Great Awakening

o. Underground Railroad

p. *Uncle Tom's Cabin*

q. Mormon

r. Compromise of 1850

s. railroad

t. Fugitive Slave Law

Complete these items (each answer, 2 points).

41. Name three areas in which reformers were active in the early 1800s.

    a. _____

    b. _____

    c. _____

42. What two parties did the Democratic-Republican Party split into?

    a. _____

    b. _____

43. Name the law that ended the era of compromise and the man who created it.

    a. _____

    b. _____

44. Who was the only president of this era to serve two terms?

    _____

45. Name one of the reasons for the Panic of 1837.

    _____

46. Why did California's population grow so quickly after 1848?

    _____

80 / 100

Date _____

Score _____

Name _____

Match these items (each item, 2 points).

1. _____ almost started a war between the Union and Britain when Confederates taken off it

2. _____ ". . . government of the people, by the people, for the people shall not perish from this earth."

3. _____ south was divided into five military districts

4. _____ the worst effects of popular sovereignty

5. _____ almost cost Grant his military career

6. _____ ended the pre-Civil War era of compromise

7. _____ made slavery legal in all states

8. _____ beginning of the Civil War

9. _____ British raider with a Confederate flag

10. _____ John Brown's act of martyrdom

11. _____ end of Lee's army

12. _____ end of the last southern invasion of the north

13. _____ railroad construction scandal

14. _____ Confederate ironclad

15. _____ post-war laws to subjugate Freedmen

16. _____ ended slavery

17. _____ gave Republicans the presidency in exchange for the end of Reconstruction

18. _____ made former slaves citizens

19. _____ insured that anti-slavery Britain would not aid the Confederacy

20. _____ bribery used to cheat government out of excise revenue

a. Dred Scott Decision

b. Battle of Gettysburg

c. Fort Sumter

d. Kansas-Nebraska Act

e. Black Codes

f. 13th Amendment

g. Emancipation Proclamation

h. Radical Reconstruction

i. Compromise of 1877

j. 14th Amendment

k. *Trent*

l. *Alabama*

m. *Merrimac*

n. Appomattox Courthouse

o. Gettysburg Address

p. Whiskey Ring

q. Crédit Mobilier

r. Bleeding Kansas

s. Harper's Ferry Raid

t. Shiloh

Name the president (each answer, 3 points).

21. _____ little formal education, excellent speaker, assassinated

22. _____ pro-south, did nothing to stop secession

23. _____ poor president, corrupt administration, Civil War memoirs provided for his family

24. _____ never elected president, former tailor, did not secede with his state

25. _____ governor of Ohio, favored civil service reform, election questionable

Name the person (each answer, 2 points).

Robert E. Lee	Stephen Douglas	John Crittendon
Ulysses S. Grant	William Seward	Jefferson Davis
David Farragut	Stonewall Jackson	Thaddeus Stevens	William T. Sherman

26. _____ most brilliant general in the Civil War

27. _____ president of the Confederacy

28. _____ admiral who captured Mobile and New Orleans

29. _____ leader of the Radical Republicans

30. _____ Lee's brilliant subordinate, killed at Chancellorsville

31. _____ Lincoln's Democratic opponent, favored popular sovereignty

32. _____ marched to the sea, Union general

33. _____ bought Alaska for the U.S.

34. _____ victor at Petersburg

35. _____ tried to compromise to save the Union after secession began

Answer these questions (each answer, 4 points).

36. Why did the South expect Britain to support them and why (outside of slavery) did they not do so?

_____

_____

_____

37. How did Congress arrange to impeach Johnson and what was the result?

_____

_____

_____

38. Why were the number of battle deaths so high in the Civil War?

_____

_____

_____

39. What were the south's main advantages in the Civil War?

_____

_____

_____

40. What is a hard money policy and how does it affect a depression?

_____

_____

_____

Answer *true* **or** *false* (each answer, 1 point).

41. _____ The north won the war largely because it had greater resources than the south.

42. _____ Antietam allowed Lincoln to issue the Emancipation Proclamation after a Union victory.

43. _____ First Bull Run, Chancellorsville, and Fredricksburg were Union victories.

44. _____ The election of 1864 was remarkable because Lincoln almost lost in spite of the war being very popular.

45. _____ The Civil War settled the issues of the civil right of black Americans and the power of industry in America.

Date _____

Score _____

Name _____

Match these people (each answer, 2 points).

1.	_____ professional inventor: light bulb, phonograph	a. Theodore Roosevelt
2.	_____ Wilson would not recognize his government in Mexico	b. James Garfield
3.	_____ first powered airplane flight	c. Grover Cleveland
4.	_____ Democratic leader, 3 time presidential candidate, Wilson's Secretary of State	d. William J. Bryan
5.	_____ 1st Democratic president after Civil War, two non-consecutive terms	e. William H. Taft
6.	_____ his assassination encouraged civil service reform	f. Chester A. Arthur
7.	_____ made the Model T cheap enough for most Americans	g. Woodrow Wilson
8.	_____ famous American writer, author of *Gilded Age*	h. William McKinley
9.	_____ Republican Half-Breed leader, presidential candidate	i. Andrew Carnegie
10.	_____ union leader and organizer	j. Thomas Edison
11.	_____ president, got tariff reduction and banking reform	k. John D. Rockefeller
12.	_____ attacked town in New Mexico, pursued into Mexico	l. James Blaine
13.	_____ chosen as Roosevelt's successor, preferred to be a judge	m. Henry Ford
14.	_____ president, Billion Dollar Congress, Sherman Anti-Trust	n. Wright brothers
15.	_____ worker in Roscoe Conkling's political machine, surprisingly pushed civil service reform as president	o. Robert La Follette
16.	_____ Progressive leader, Wisconsin governor	p. Samuel Gompers
17.	_____ Standard Oil Trust, squashed competitors	q. Benjamin Harrison
18.	_____ made fortune in steel, gave most of it away	r. Mark Twain
19.	_____ pro-business president, front porch campaign, tried to avoid war with Spain, assassinated	s. Pancho Villa
20.	_____ first Progressive president, served in Spanish-American War, extremely popular	t. Victoriano Huerta

Answer these questions (each answer, 3 points).

21. Why did America change its policy of no government interference in business?

_____

22.   What was the reform party that proceeded the Progressives and nominated Byran?

        _____

23.   How did Theodore Roosevelt arrange for a canal treaty after Colombia refused it?

        _____

        _____

24.   Progressive reforms began at what level of government?

        _____

25.   Why was Gilded Age a good description of the period of 1865 to 1900?

        _____

        _____

26.   Why did Woodrow Wilson win the 1912 election?

        _____

Match these items (each answer, 2 points).

27.   _____ craft unions, pro-capitalist, pushed wages and conditions   a. muckrakers

28.   _____ exposed unsanitary meat packing conditions   b. laissez-faire

29.   _____ poor are unfit and deserve poverty   c. Pendleton Act

30.   _____ TR's policy to accomplish results   d. Big Stick

31.   _____ helped rapid settlement of Great Plains   e. Knights of Labor

32.   _____ gave Indian families land   f. AFL

33.   _____ U.S. intervened in Americas to stop Europe
             from intervening   g. Grange

34.   _____ Bryan's famous convention speech, 1896   h. *Cross of Gold*

35.   _____ sought debt relief and railroad regulation   i. imperialism

36.   _____ 1st major U.S. union movement, discredited
             by Haymarket Riot   j. *The Jungle*

37.   _____ expanded American influence by investments abroad   k. Dawes Act

38.   _____ major political issue right after Spanish-American War   l. Homestead Act

39.   _____ government should interfere as little as possible
             with business   m. Social Darwinism

40.   _____ federal civil service reform   n. Roosevelt Corollary

41.   _____ writers who exposed corruption or social problems   o. Dollar Diplomacy

Write *true* **or** *false* **in the blank** (each answer, 1 point).

42. _____ Theodore Roosevelt started more anti-trust suits than Taft.

43. _____ The New Immigration of the 1870s and 80s came from central Asia.

44. _____ The U.S. had a transcontinental railroad since before the Civil War.

45. _____ The Plains Indians put up stiff resistance to American settlers.

46. _____ Railroads, before regulation, had tremendous, arbitrary control over the profitability of businesses and farmers that depended on rail shipment.

47. _____ Immigrants were not hired as industrial workers because they did not understand American business practices.

48. _____ In the late 1800s, unions were opposed by owners, courts, and the government.

49. _____ Woodrow Wilson won the Nobel Peace Prize for his handling of the crisis with Mexico.

50. _____ The poorer working people hooked onto the issue of silver coinage as their issue in the late 1800s.

51. _____ Wilson sent the American navy, the Great White Fleet, on a tour of the world to showcase American strength.

52. _____ One problem of a gold standard was keeping enough gold reserves.

53. _____ Much of the 1888 budget surplus was given away in liberal pensions to Civil War veterans.

Date _____

Score _____

Name _____

Match these items. "WWI" will be used as an abbreviation for World War I and "WWII" for World War II (each answer, 2 points).

1. _____ Revolution in Russia, pulled it out of WWI
2. _____ Island fortress, Manila Bay
3. _____ Trial on evolution education, ridiculed Christianity
4. _____ Volcanic island between Japan and Mariana Islands, taken by the Marines in 1944
5. _____ Largest American attack of WWI
6. _____ Japanese navy's fighting effectiveness ended, WWII
7. _____ American strategy in Pacific, WWII
8. _____ Wilson's liberal peace plan
9. _____ WWI Veterans, needing money in 1932, marched on Washington
10. _____ Turning point in Europe, WWII
11. _____ Ended WWI, set up WWII
12. _____ Gave Hitler the countries he wanted without a fight before WWII
13. _____ Young men did conservation work for small wages
14. _____ Killed more Americans than WWI did in 1918-19
15. _____ Scandal under Warren G. Harding
16. _____ Section of the economy in trouble in early 1920s
17. _____ Declared by F.D.R. right after his inauguration
18. _____ Triggered the Great Depression
19. _____ U.S. fought wolf packs to get supplies to Britain
20. _____ 6 million deaths in Nazi concentration camps
21. _____ Hitler's last major offensive
22. _____ Destroyed Hiroshima and Nagasaki
23. _____ First British victory of WWII, N. Africa
24. _____ Location of Allied invasion of France, WWII
25. _____ F.D.R.'s plan to fight the Great Depression

a. Battle of the Bulge
b. Battle of the Atlantic
c. Battle of Leyte Gulf
d. Meuse-Argonne Offensive
e. Agriculture
f. Stock Market Crash
g. Scopes Monkey Trial
h. Atomic bombs
i. Treaty of Versailles
j. CCC
k. El Alamein
l. Normandy
m. Iwo Jima
n. New Deal
o. Island hopping
p. Bonus Army
q. Corregidor
r. Holocaust
s. Communist
t. Tea Pot Dome
u. Bank holiday
v. Influenza
w. Fourteen Points
x. Appeasement
y. Stalingrad

Name the person (each answer, 3 points).

26. _____ Supreme commander of Allied forces in Europe, WWII

27. _____ President of the U.S., WWI

28. _____ U.S. general who lost and recaptured the Philippines, WWII

29. _____ Dictator of Germany, WWII

30. _____ Prime Minister of Britain during most of WWII

31. _____ Commander American Expeditionary Force, WWI

32. _____ President who was blamed for the Great Depression

33. _____ Fascist dictator of Italy, WWII

34. _____ Communist dictator of the U.S.S.R., WWII

35. _____ Austrian heir, assassination began WWI

Write *true* **or** *false* **on the blank.** If the answer is false, change a word or phrase to make it true. **Note:** Putting the word "not" into the sentence is insufficient (each answer, 2 points).

36. _____ During World War I, the front was mainly a stalemate of blitzkrieg warfare.

37. _____ At the height of the Great Depression, 50% of all Americans were out of work.

38. _____ The Zimmerman note pushed America to get involved in World War I.

39. _____ After World War I, the main goal of France was to be sure Germany became a free and stable democracy.

40. _____ Immediately after the fall of France in World War II, only the Soviet Union was still fighting Germany.

41. _____ Charles de Gaulle was a Free French leader and Chiang Kai-shek was a Japanese leader.

42. _____ Charles Lindbergh was famous for being the first person to fly an airplane across the Atlantic alone.

43. _____ The Ku Klux Klan became popular during the years after World War I.

44. _____ Prohibition was an attempt from 1919 to 1932 to outlaw cigarettes.

It failed.

45. _____ The first major military action by America in Europe during World War II

was the invasion of Sicily.

Date _____

Score _____

Name _____

Match each event, scandal, or crisis with its description. Then, on the line after the description, name the president(s) during the event. Some presidents will be used more than once (each answer—matching and president's name—is worth 2 points).

1. _____ Navy task force sent in to rescue U.S. merchant ship seized by Cambodia _____

2. _____ Korean commander had public approval when he disagreed with his superiors _____

3. _____ Attempt to "bug" the Democrats and a cover up of White House involvement _____

4. _____ Attack by the North Vietnamese at New Year's that proved they were still strong _____

5. _____ The U.S.S.R. said it would no longer defend Iron Curtain governments, 1989 _____

6. _____ Cuban exiles failed to overthrow Castro in an attempt the U.S. did not fully support _____

7. _____ Iraqi army was driven out of Kuwait in a 100 hour ground war _____

8. _____ U.S. ship allegedly attacked; gave the president a free hand in Vietnam _____

9. _____ Set up in San Francisco in 1945, Security Council makes major decisions _____

10. _____ Embassy staff held for 444 days, U.S. military rescue fails _____

11. _____ North attacked the south, drove them back to the Pusan Perimeter, conflict ended by a cease fire, not a treaty
(a) _____ (b) _____

12. _____ U.S. spy plane shot down over the U.S.S.R., pilot captured
_____

13. _____ Noriega invalidated an election, was indicted for drug trafficking, and unrest endangered American soldiers _____

14. _____ Weapons were sold to a terrorist nation to gain the release of hostages, profits from the sale were used to finance anti-communist rebels in Central America
_____

15. _____ Naval blockade set up to prevent the arrival of Soviet nuclear weapons, Soviets did not challenge it _____

a. Iran Hostage Crisis

b. U-2 Affair

c. Bay of Pigs

d. Gulf of Tonkin Resolution

e. Korean War

f. Firing of MacArthur

g. Watergate

h. *Mayaguez*

i. Iran-Contra Affair

j. Persian Gulf War

k. United Nations

m. Fall of Communism in Europe

n. Invasion of Panama

o. Tet Offensive

p. Cuban Missile Crisis

Name the item, event, or person (each answer, 3 points).

16.   Conflict of ideas, economics, propaganda and intimidation between the U.S. and the U.S.S.R. from 1945 to 1991 _____

17.   Reform movement that began with the Montgomery bus boycott led by Martin Luther King in 1955 _____

18.   The main policy of the U.S. toward communism from 1945 to 1991

    _____

19.   American aid given to rebuild Europe after World War II

    _____

20.   America's biggest economic problem after World War II until the early 1980s

    _____

21.   Man who began *perestroika* and *glasnost* in the Soviet Union in the 1980s

    _____

22.   Thaw in relations between America and the Soviet Union in the 1970s

    _____

23.   Volunteer organization set up by Kennedy to aid Third World nations

    _____

24.   Segregation policy <u>ended</u> by *Brown v. Board of Education of Topeka*

    _____

25.   Nation in which Pol Pot and the Khmer Rouge killed over a million people

    _____

26.   Joseph McCarthy accused many people of this

    _____

Answer *true* **or** *false* (each answer, 1 point).

27.   _____ The Vietnam War helped America recover from the failure in Korea.

28.   _____ Jimmy Carter was the first president to visit the U.S.S.R.

29.   _____ The fear of nuclear weapons is one important reason why America and the Soviet Union never went to war with each other.

30.   _____ The Soviet Union was the early leader in space exploration.

31.   _____ Mao Zedong and Communist China became American allies right after World War II to counter Soviet influence in Korea.

Date _____

Score _____

History & Geography 810 Alternate Test

Name _____

Answer these questions (each answer, 3 points).

1. What were the weaknesses of the Articles of Confederation? _____
   _____

2. Why were so many colonies settled from Massachusetts? _____
   _____

3. What were the causes of World War I? _____
   _____

4. Why was the Vietnam War controversial? _____
   _____

5. What was the legacy of the Federalists? _____
   _____

6. What were the causes of the War of 1812? _____
   _____

7. What was the Cold War? _____
   _____

8. What was the Industrial Revolution? _____
   _____

9. What caused the Great Depression? _____
   _____

10. What advantages did the South have in the Civil War? _____
    _____

Put these events in chronological order (20 points, take off only one point for every event out of order).

11. _____ Founding of Virginia
12. _____ Impeachment of Clinton
13. _____ Vietnam War protests
14. _____ Exploration of Coronado
15. _____ Stamp Act
16. _____ Declaration of Independence
17. _____ Gettysburg Address
18. _____ Korean War
19. _____ Battle of the Bulge
20. _____ Attack on Fort Sumter

21. _____ The Crusades
22. _____ Impeachment of Johnson
23. _____ Kansas-Nebraska Act
24. _____ *Common Sense*
25. _____ Constitutional Convention
26. _____ Missouri Compromise
27. _____ Berlin Airlift
28. _____ Battle of New Orleans
29. _____ Appomattox Courthouse
30. _____ Fourteen Points

Match these items (each answer, 2 points).

31. _____ Largest American battle of WWI

32. _____ Civil War generals

33. _____ Training ground for the Civil War, acquired California

34. _____ The Alamo, San Jacinto

35. _____ Progressive presidents

36. _____ America's first permanent alliance since the Revolution

37. _____ Area settled by Puritans, fishing and shipbuilding

38. _____ First 10 amendments to the Constitution

39. _____ Presidents who were assassinated

40. _____ Henry Clay

41. _____ Last, decisive battle of the Revolutionary War

42. _____ Dominant power in North America after 1793

43. _____ Turning point of the Revolutionary War

44. _____ Poor presidents with corrupt administrations

45. _____ WWII generals

46. _____ Vastly reduced shipping costs from the
Great Lakes to New York City

47. _____ Had the best relations with the Indians in
N. America, America's ally in the Revolution

48. _____ Freed the slaves in the rebellious states, 1862

49. _____ Revival in colonial America

50. _____ Conflict to free Kuwait from Iraq

51. _____ Gilded Age presidents

52. _____ Cold War presidents

53. _____ Turning point of the Pacific War, WWII

54. _____ Scandal that forced President Nixon to resign

55. _____ Economic theory of the 1700s, colonies should
benefit the mother country

a. T. Roosevelt, Taft, Wilson

b. Saratoga

c. Mexican War

d. Persian Gulf War

e. Great Compromiser

f. Harding & Grant

g. Erie Canal

h. Garfield, McKinley, Kennedy

i. Texas Revolution

j. Great Awakening

k. Truman, Johnson, Nixon

l. Meuse-Argonne

m. Midway

n. Yorktown

o. Mercantilism

p. Arthur, Cleveland, Hayes

q. NATO

r. Lee, Sherman, Grant

s. MacArthur, Patton, Eisenhower

t. France

u. New England

v. Bill of Rights

w. Emancipation Proclamation

x. Britain

y. Watergate

Bonus: On a separate piece of paper, list the last 23 presidents of the United States, following James Garfield and Chester A. Arthur. (10 points maximum)

Date _____

Score _____

LIFEPAC

ANSWER KEYS

SECTION ONE

1.1 Any order:
   a. Rome
   b. Greece
   c. Jews
   d. Christianity

1.2 Asia, across the Bering Strait

1.3 Either order:
   a. Crusades
   b. Marco Polo's book

1.4 Trade from the contact with Asia led to improved ships, education, larger cities, and stronger governments.

1.5 A.D. 476, Medieval

1.6 Roman Catholic Church

1.7 Seljuk Turks

1.8 China

1.9 Any order:
   a. long trade routes over land and sea
   b. land routes controlled by Muslims
   c. Italian monopoly on the trade

1.10 Either order:
   a. find the source of African gold
   b. find a route to Asia

1.11 false (change *Spain* to *Portugal*)

1.12 true

1.13 false (change *alchemy* to *geography*)

1.14 true

1.15 false (change *Bartholomeu Diaz* to *Vasco da Gama*)

1.16 true

1.17 Genoa

1.18 west

1.19 half

1.20 Any order: Portugal, France, England

1.21 Any order: Ferdinand, Isabella

1.22 Muslim, Granada

1.23 Any order: *Niña, Pinta, Santa Maria*

1.24 He believed his own experts who said the earth was larger than Columbus' estimates and he did not want to grant the explorer's demands for himself.

1.25 Either order:
   a. on the island of Hispaniola
   b. Columbus

1.26 four

1.27 yes, Central America is part of North America

1.28 Amerigo Vespucci

1.29 That they were in or near Asia

1.30 Vikings under Leif Ericson

1.31 It established permanent contact between the Americas and Europe.

1.32 Ponce de León

1.33 Balboa

1.34 Ponce de León

1.35 Magellan

1.36 Coronado

1.37 Pizarro

1.38 Magellan

1.39 De Soto

1.40 Cortes

1.41 Coronado

1.42 De Soto

1.43 Spain and Portugal

1.44 To divide the non-Christian lands of the world "fairly" between the two

1.45 Line of Demarcation

1.46 They were soldiers and noblemen who came to get rich. They explored, mapped, and conquered much of the Americas for Spain.

1.47 Any order:
   a. America was a long way from Asia
   b. the world is a sphere

1.48 Any order
   a. Spain concentrated its attention on Mexico and South America
   b. the treasure excited the interest of the other nations of Europe

1.49 Teacher check

SECTION TWO

2.1 Henry VII

2.2 John Cabot

2.3 Sir Francis Drake

2.4 Elizabeth I

2.5 Grand Banks

2.6 Invincible Armada

2.7 He gave England a claim to North America along Canada and the eastern United States as well as discovering the Grand Banks.

2.8 They kept the Spanish fleet busy, reduced Spain's profit, and gave Elizabeth income.

2.9 He attacked Spanish interests on the American west coast, explored the west coast of North America, and captured a great deal of treasure.

2.10 The defeat of the Invincible Armada, pirate attacks, rebellions in Spanish lands, bad management, and over-spending.

2.11 false (change *Northeast* to *Northwest*)

2.12 false (new wording: *three* times for England and *one* time for the Netherlands)

2.13 true

2.14 false (change Hudson *Bay* to Hudson *River*)

2.15 true

2.16 false (change the *United States* to *Canada*)

2.17 They were fishermen who came to fish the Grand Banks and dry their catch on land.

2.18 The Gulf of St. Lawrence and the St. Lawrence River.

2.19 St. Lawrence River, Great Lakes, the east coast south to Massachusetts, northern New York

2.20 The Iroquois became enemies of France, allies with England, and interfered with French settlements south of the Great Lakes

2.21 yes

2.22 no

2.23 no

2.24 no

2.25 no

2.26 *coureus de bois*

2.27 fur

2.28 Mississippi

2.29 Asia

2.30 landowner, fur

2.31 Louisiana

2.32 Down the Fox River from Lake Michigan to the Wisconsin River, south to the Mississippi until the Arkansas River, back up the Mississippi to the Illinois and Chicago River, and back to Lake Michigan

2.33 South of the Great Lakes around the Ohio River, the Mississippi River, and part of Texas on the Gulf of Mexico

2.34 All of the Mississippi Basin, from the Appalachians to the Rocky Mountains

SECTION THREE

3.1 false (change *California* to *Florida*)
3.2 false (change *Santa Fe* to *St. Augustine*)
3.3 true
3.4 true
3.5 false (change *San Diego* to *Santa Fe*)
3.6 false (new wording: governor *appointed* by the *king*)
3.7 true
3.8 false (change *America* to *Spain*)
3.9 true
3.10 Dutch
3.11 French
3.12 French
3.13 Dutch
3.14 French
3.15 Strict government control of politics and trade, land held by rich landowners, and no religious freedom
3.16 The French needed the Indians to trap furs and the small French population was less of a threat to the Indians
3.17 The Dutch West India Company
3.18 Huge tracts of land were given to company members who brought over fifty people to settle on it.
3.19 They were ruled over by a privileged land-owning aristocracy and despotic governors who were appointed by the West India Company and were often poor administrators.
3.20 Any order: Humphrey Gilbert, Walter Raleigh
3.21 Any order: 1585, 1587
3.22 Virginia Dare
3.23 king
3.24 John Smith
3.25 Algonquin, Powhatan
3.26 Pocahontas
3.27 It disappeared without a trace while the leader was in England for three years.
3.28 Roanoke was sponsored by an individual nobleman while Jamestown's sponsor was a joint stock company.

3.29 It was chosen because it was an easily defendable peninsula but it was swampy and subjected the men to disease.
3.30 Any order:
   a. lack of unity
   b. inferior weapons
   c. lack of immunity to European diseases
   d. Europeans kept coming
3.31 Too many settlers arrived. They overwhelmed the food and shelter resources of the colony. Most of the people starved to death.
3.32 Every settler in Virginia was given 50 acres of land if he stayed three years.
3.33 Any order:
   a. House of Burgesses meets
   b. boatload of women sent from England
   c. first African slaves arrive
3.34 About three hundred and fifty colonists were killed, the London Company lost its charter, Virginia became a crown colony
3.35 Almost 500 colonists were killed, the power of the Virginia Indians was broken and they were confined to reservations
3.36 tobacco
3.37 An indentured servant is a bound for a term of years and is then free. A slave is bound for life unless freed by his master.
3.38 Pocahontas
3.39 Any order:
   a. Spain: Florida, Mexico, and the southwest U.S.
   b. France: St. Lawrence, Great Lakes, Mississippi Basin
   c. England: U.S. east coast, Hudson Bay area

SECTION ONE

1.1 Puritans wanted to stay in the Anglican church and purify it. Separatists wanted to leave it.

1.2 Separatists

1.3 They were arrested after having their goods stolen by a dishonest captain. On the second try, the women and children were arrested when the men were on the ship.

1.4 They did not want their children to become Dutch, and they feared a Dutch-Spanish war.

1.5 It leaked.

1.6 Overcrowding, foul conditions, lack of exercise, no fresh air

1.7 They were at Cape Cod, north of Virginia. They only had permission to settle in Virginia.

1.8 For the glory of God, to advance the Christian faith, to honor their king and country

1.9 God and each other

1.10 Ireland–18 years; Scotland–54 years

1.11 They agreed to form a "Civil Body Politic"–a government, to establish laws which they promised to obey for the better ordering and preservation of the colony

1.12 b

1.13 e

1.14 d

1.15 a

1.16 c

1.17 false

1.18 true

1.19 false

1.20 false

1.21 true

1.22 true

1.23 Teacher check

1.24 Charles I

1.25 William Laud

1.26 Massachusetts Bay

1.27 John Winthrop

1.28 Puritan

1.29 Anne Hutchinson

1.30 The charter did not specify that the company must meet in England. So, the company moved to America–charter and all.

1.31 The assembly was elected by the church members who owned property.

1.32 false, Fundamental Orders of Conn.

1.33 true

1.34 false; Hartford

1.35 false; Indians, should not be

1.36 true

1.37 true

1.38 false; parliament

1.39 true

1.40 true

1.41 false; Massachusetts

1.42 New York

1.43 New York, New Jersey

1.44 New Jersey, Delaware, Pennsylvania

1.45 New Jersey, Delaware, Pennsylvania

1.46 New York

1.47 New Jersey

1.48 New Jersey

1.49 New York

1.50   New York

1.51   New Jersey

1.52   New Jersey

1.53   To settle a debt the king owed to Penn's father

1.54   Interference from the Duke of York and colonists who would not pay quitrents

1.55   Charles II gave the land to his brother, the Duke of York, who sent four ships to capture it. They did so without firing a shot.

1.56   A religious sect that were pacifists, emphasized an "inner light," did not take oaths, or pay taxes to the Anglican church

1.57   Pennsylvania

1.58   Maryland

1.59   Georgia

1.60   Carolinas

1.61   Maryland

1.62   Georgia

1.63   South Carolina

1.64   North Carolina

1.65   Georgia

1.66   Carolinas

1.67   South Carolina

1.68   Georgia

1.69   Maryland

1.70   Maryland

1.71   Georgia

1.72   Maryland

1.73   Georgia

1.74   false; South Carolina

1.75   true

1.76   false; Catholics

1.77   true

1.78   false; Spanish Florida

1.79   false; eight

SECTION TWO

2.1   a. Massachusetts, Virginia

    b. Connecticut, Rhode Island

    c. Maryland, North and South Carolina, New Hampshire, New York, New Jersey, Georgia, Delaware, Pennsylvania

2.2   a. none

    b. Connecticut, Rhode Island

    c. Pennsylvania, Delaware, Maryland

    d. North and South Carolina, New Hampshire, New York, New Jersey, Georgia, Virginia, Massachusetts

2.3   Land was owned by the nobles who rented it to farmers.

2.4   The farmers could get land elsewhere if they did not want to pay rent.

2.5   a. Governor; veto laws, appoint officials, lead council, pardon criminals, control militia, handle both diplomatic and religious affairs

    b. council; highest court, approve laws, assist governor

    c. assembly; control finances, write laws

2.6   a. supervision by Board of Trade

b. most governors let assembly do the work

c. assembly controlled the money

2.7   after the French and Indian War, 1760s

2.8   true

2.9   false

2.10 true

2.11 false

2.12 true

2.13 false

2.14 true

2.15 a. fishing

b. whaling

c. shipbuilding

2.16 a. so that people could learn to read the Bible and thwart Satan

b. when it had fifty households

c. all children that came

2.17 wheat

2.18 the West Indies

2.19 tobacco

2.20 Any order: rice, indigo

2.21 indentured servants; African slaves

2.22 Philadelphia

2.23 southern

2.24 trade; farming

2.25 Middle

2.26 high wages

2.27 Charleston

2.28 plantations

2.29 slave holding; plantation

2.30 Any order: Jonathan Edwards, George Whitefield

2.31 Any order: Congregationalists, Anglicans

2.32 Any order: Rhode Island, Pennsylvania, Delaware, New Jersey

2.33 Halfway

2.34 Salem witch

2.35 Deism

2.36 *Sinners in the Hands of an Angry God*

2.37 taxes

2.38 pastors

2.39 Teacher check if student understands the event

2.40 c

2.41 b

2.42 b

2.43 a

2.44 d

2.45 e

2.46 e

2.47 a

2.48 e

2.49 c

2.50 a

2.51 d

2.52 d

2.53 e

2.54 c

2.55 b

SECTION THREE

3.1   a. King William's War;
               War of the Grand Alliance (or
               League of Augsburg)
      b. Queen Anne's War;
               War of the Spanish Succession
      c. King George's War;
               War of the Austrian Succession

3.2   War of Jenkin's Ear

3.3   a

3.4   a

3.5   c

3.6   a ,b

3.7   a, b

3.8   c

3.9   b

3.10 d

3.11 b

3.12 b

3.13 b

3.14 b

3.15 British

3.16 British

3.17 British

3.18 French

3.19 French

3.20 French

3.21 a

3.22 b

3.23 b

3.24 c

3.25 a

3.26 b

3.27 a

3.28 b

3.29 c

3.30 c

3.31 a

3.32 b

3.33 a

3.34 a. gave gifts to the Iroquois and
               encouraged them to be loyal to
               Britain
      b. Put together a plan for a united
               colonial government

3.35 a. Oswego
      b. William Henry

3.36 Seven Years

3.37 b

3.38 c

3.39 d

3.40 false

3.41 true

3.42 false

3.43 false

3.44 true

3.45 ✔

3.46

3.47 ✔

3.48

3.49

3.50 ✔

3.51 ✔

3.52 ✔

3.53 ✔

3.54 a. fur trade
      b. farming

3.55 British took land for farming while
       French only built forts and traded.

3.56 To destroy the frontier forts and then
       attack the unprotected settlers

3.57 All along the British frontier

3.58 They began to run out of supplies.

3.59 No settlers west of the Appalachians,
       land there must be bought from the
       Indians or obtained by treaty

3.60 They ignored it.

3.61 Teacher check

SECTION ONE

1.1 mercantilism

1.2 supply the mother country with raw materials and buy manufactured goods from her

1.3 Any order:
   a. bring them under better control
   b. have them pay some of the cost of running the colonies

1.4 Any order:
   a. All trade on British or colonial ships
   b. All trade must go through Britain
   c. Certain goods could be sold only to Britain

1.5 The Molasses Act set a high tax on non-British molasses. It would have hurt New England because the British source for molasses (British West Indies) could not supply all that New England needed. It was avoided by smuggling.

1.6 The colonies were not allowed to mint coins nor could colonial goods be purchased with coins from Britain.

1.7 1763-strict enforcement of the Navigation Acts
   1764-Sugar Act
   1765-Quartering Act

1.8 Grenville

1.9 Benjamin Franklin

1.10 Patrick Henry

1.11 Virginia Resolves

1.12 Any order:
   a. Stamp Act Congress
   b. boycotts
   c. mob action

1.13 Sons of Liberty

1.14 "No taxation without representation."

1.15 Declaratory Act

1.16 A stamp had to be purchased for all legal and public papers: like wills, bills of sale, and even playing cards.

1.17 Any four: first direct tax, tax fell on everyone, it was not passed by the colonial assemblies, violators would be tried in Admiralty Court, and colonists were already short of money

1.18 Those men killed the tyrants they opposed. George III might face the same fate if he continued to act as a tyrant.

1.19 false, change *France* to *England*

1.20 false, change *Prime Minister* to *Chancellor of the Exchequer*

1.21 true

1.22 false, change *Massachusetts* to *New York* and *Stamp* to *Quartering*

1.23 true

1.24 false, change *colonial assemblies* to *Parliament*

1.25 true

1.26 false, change *West* to *North* and *paint* to *tea*

1.27 true

1.28 true

1.29 Tax on goods from Britain like tea,
lead, and paint; gave greater powers of enforcement to customs officials; revenue to be used to pay British officials

1.30 A mob threw snowballs and debris at soldiers. The soldiers fired and five people were killed.

1.31 British East India Company

1.32 Charleston

1.33 New York

1.34 Boston Port

1.35 Quebec

1.36 First Continental Congress

1.37 Boston Tea Party

1.38 Closed Boston harbor, restricted town meeting, important official put under royal control, Boston put under military rule

1.39 A group of colonists, disguised as Indians took the tea off of ships in the harbor and dumped it into the ocean.

1.40 It passed a Declaration of Rights, declared several acts of Parliament illegal, formed an association to stop all trade, petitioned the king, and agreed to meet again if necessary.

1.41 It took away the Ohio land, spread Catholicism, and was a further attempt to contain their liberties.

1.42 b

1.43 a

1.44 c

1.45 b

1.46 c

1.47 a

1.48 a

1.49 b

1.50 c

1.51 c

1.52 a

1.53 b

1.54 c

1.55 Second Continental Congress

1.56 militia

1.57 George Washington

1.58 d

1.59 e

1.60 b

1.61 f

1.62 a

1.63 c

1.64 g

1.65 Olive Branch

1.66 Montreal

1.67 *Common Sense*

1.68 July 2, 1776

1.69 15

1.70 first two paragraphs

1.71 a. "He has refused . . ."
b. ". . . in Peace Friends."

1.72 last

1.73 Teacher check

1.74-1.84 (teacher may approve alternate answers)

1.74 "He has dissolved Representative Houses repeatedly"

1.75 "He has refused his Assent to Laws"

1.76 "He has made Judges dependent on his will alone"

1.77 "For imposing taxes on us without our consent"

1.78 "For depriving us . . . of the benefits of Trial by Jury"

1.79 "For taking away our Charters . . . and altering fundamentally the Forms of our Government"

1.80 "For cutting off our Trade with all parts of the world"

1.81 "has endeavoured to bring on the inhabitants of our frontiers, the merciless Indian Savages"

1.82 "transporting large armies of foreign Mercenaries to compleat the works of death"

1.83 "For Quartering large bodies of armed troops among us"

1.84 "to render the military independent of and superior to the Civil Power"

1.85 "For abolishing the free System of English Laws in a neighbouring Province . . . and enlarging its Boundaries"

SECTION TWO

2.1	British	2.27	e
2.2	British	2.28	a
2.3	Americans	2.29	b
2.4	British	2.30	a
2.5	Americans	2.31	f
2.6	Americans	2.32	e
2.7	British	2.33	f
2.8	British	2.34	a
2.9	Americans	2.35	d
2.10	British	2.36	e
2.11	Keeping the army together	2.37	a
2.12	cannons from Ticonderoga	2.38	f
2.13	The British withdrew and had to start from Canada, not New York, in 1777.	2.39	c
		2.40	Burgoyne, St. Leger, Howe
2.14	It failed and the south was left alone for awhile	2.41	Fort Stanwix, Oriskany Creek
		2.42	Ticonderoga, Defiance
2.15	They were attacked from the front and rear. They were defeated and fled to Brooklyn Heights.	2.43	30, cannons
		2.44	Jane McCrea
		2.45	Bennington
2.16	An American officer who was collecting information, was caught, and hanged as a spy.	2.46	Freeman's Farm
		2.47	Any order: Benedict Arnold, Daniel Morgan
2.17	The British captured them.	2.48	Horatio Gates
2.18	Washington snuck away in small boats at night.	2.49	Saratoga
		2.50	Saratoga
2.19	Very poor. They had little food or supplies.	2.51	Any order: Saratoga, Germantown
		2.52	Marquis de Lafayette
2.20	It is not easily conquered.	2.53	Benjamin Franklin
2.21	God	2.54	Monmouth Courthouse
2.22	summer soldiers and sunshine patriots	2.55	George Rogers Clark
2.23	esteem it too lightly	2.56	Vincennes
2.24	b	2.57	Benedict Arnold, West Point
2.25	c	2.58	Charles Lee
2.26	e		

2.59 John Paul Jones, *Bonhomme Richard*, *Serapis*

2.60 Major John André

2.61 d

2.62 b

2.63 c

2.64 a

2.65 g

2.66 e

2.67 f

2.68 Francis Marion

2.69 Daniel Morgan

2.70 Nathanael Greene

2.71 Horatio Gates

2.72 Lord Cornwallis

2.73 A French fleet cut off his supply and retreat route. A combined French and American army surrounded him by land.

2.74 Rochambeau

2.75 de Grasse

2.76 Ben Franklin, John Adams, John Jay

2.77 General Benjamin Lincoln

2.78 It prevented America from falling under a military dictatorship and gave the country a tremendous confidence in Washington that would be used later.

2.79 Any order:
1. Independence for America
2. America got all the land between Canada and Florida east of the Mississippi
3. British troops to leave
4. Americans could use the Mississippi
5. Americans could fish in Newfoundland
6. Spain got Florida back
7. France got back its islands in the West Indies
8. Congress recommended that Loyalists get their property back
9. All debts to Britain were to be honored

SECTION THREE

3.1

3.2 ✔

3.3 ✔

3.4

3.5

3.6

3.7

3.8 ✔

3.9

3.10 ✔

3.11

3.12

3.13 Northwest Ordinance

3.14 national government

3.15 national debt

3.16 six miles, six miles

3.17 36; 16

3.18 60,000

3.19 false, change *creditors* to *debtors*

3.20 false, change *state boundaries* to *commerce*

3.21 false, change *seven* to *five*

3.22   true

3.23   true

3.24   true

3.25   false, change *poor* to *rich*

3.26   false, change *good* to *bad*

3.27   true

3.28   false, change *same* to *different*

3.29   12

3.30   wealthy

3.31   Any order:

    a. George Washington elected president

    b. meeting would be secret

    c. throw out the Articles of Confederation

3.32   Any order:

    a. Virginia Plan–Congressional representation would be based on population

    b. New Jersey Plan–Congressional representation would be a set number per state

3.33   Connecticut Plan

3.34   Congress would have two houses, the lower one with representation by population, the upper with representation by state and money bills would start in the lower house.

3.35   Each slave would be counted as three-fifths of a person for representation and taxation purposes.

3.36   Congress could not vote to outlaw it until 1807.

3.37   Any order:

    a. executive

    b. legislative

    c. judicial

3.38   a. veto laws

    b. override veto, impeach

    c. declare laws unconstitutional

    d. appoints judges

    e. approves judges

3.39   They kept it but gave up certain powers to the federal government.

3.40   no

3.41   nine

3.42   Federalists, Anti-Federalists

3.43   Bill of Rights

3.44   Delaware

3.45   New Hampshire

3.46   Any order: Virginia, New York

3.47   Any order: North Carolina, Rhode Island

3.48   Any order:

    1. to form a more perfect union

    2. establish justice

    3. insure domestic tranquillity

    4. provide for the common defense

    5. promote the general welfare

    6. secure the blessings of liberty

SECTION ONE

1.1   c

1.2   d

1.3   e

1.4   f

1.5   b

1.6   a

1.7   Any order:
    a. pay debt at full value
    b. take over state debts
    c. National Bank

1.8   The national capital would be located in the south.

1.9   tariffs

1.10   Most of the original owners of the bonds had sold them at a small part of their value to rich people who could hold them until some payment was made on them.

1.11   H

1.12   H

1.13   J

1.14   J

1.15   J

1.16   J

1.17   H

1.18   H

1.19   Any order:
    a. stars
    b. stripes on shield
    c. olives
    d. arrows
    e. layers on pyramid

1.20   Any order:
    a. ring of golden light, obverse
    b. eye surrounded by light, reverse

1.21   The right is the more important side and it shows that America prefers peace.

1.22   "One out of many"

1.23   Neutrality Proclamation

1.24   Britain, Austria, Spain, Prussia

1.25   Citizen Edmond Genêt

1.26   Any order:
    a. commissioned privateers
    b. tried to organize expeditions against Spanish territory
    c. appealed to U.S. people to support France

1.27   Any order:
    a. holding forts in U.S. territory
    b. supporting the Indians
    c. seizing ships and cargo
    d. impressing sailors

1.28   Any order:
    a. leave the forts
    b. pay for some ships and cargo
    c. improve U.S. trading rights

1.29   It did not deal with the major issues, such as impressment; English support of the Indians or repayment for stolen slaves. It also restated the obligation of Americans to pay old debts to Britain.

1.30   It was a revolt in Pennsylvania against the excise tax. It collapsed when militia troops were sent in from out of state.

1.31   partisan politics and foreign alliances

1.32   two

1.33   Alien Act

1.34   Democratic-Republican

1.35   John Adams

1.36   Jay's Treaty

1.37   Virginia and Kentucky Resolves

1.38   Convention of 1800

1.39   XYZ Affair

1.40   Sedition Act

1.41   John Adams and Alexander Hamilton

1.42   not going to war with France

1.43   Democratic-Republican publishers

1.44 "Millions for defense but not one cent for tribute."

1.45 It was a tie between Jefferson and Burr

1.46 Jefferson, he was from a different political party.

1.47 Any order:
   a. basic structure of the government
   b. solid financial system
   c. protected the nation from early wars
   d. "loose construction" of Constitution

SECTION TWO

2.1 true

2.2 false; change *Marshall* to *Madison*

2.3 false; change *John Marshall* to *Samuel Chase*

2.4 true

2.5 false; change *unpopular* to *popular*

2.6 true

2.7 false; change *a year* to *two years*

2.8 false; change *Pocahontas* to *Sacajawea*

2.9 true

2.10 It was the first successful, peaceful change in power from one political party to another.

2.11 Nothing except to repeal the excise tax

2.12 Spain was an aging power that was very little threat and had agreed to American use of the Mississippi. France was an expanding, dangerous power.

2.13 He let them expire or repealed them, freed the men convicted under them, and returned their fines.

2.14 They ran the government as cheaply as possible while reducing the debt.

2.15 a Constitutional Amendment

2.16 Up the Missouri River, across the Rocky Mountains, and down the Columbia River

2.17 Alexander Hamilton

2.18 Austerlitz, Trafalgar

2.19 treason

2.20 *Leopard, Chesapeake*

2.21 Africa

2.22 Embargo

2.23 James Wilkinson

2.24 Orders in Council

2.25 impressment

2.26 repeal

2.27 No. It destroyed America's legitimate trade but did not seriously hurt Britain.

2.28 They demanded tribute to not capture trading ships. The pasha of Tripoli wanted a larger share and declared war.

2.29 They opposed it, calling it "O-grab-me." Illegal trade grew along the Canadian border and New England talked of leaving the Union.

2.30 A plot to separate New England, New York and New Jersey from the U.S.

2.31 James Madison

2.32 Henry Clay, John Calhoun

2.33 William Henry Harrison

2.34 Any order:
   a. wanted Canada
   b. wanted free trade
   c. wanted to end Indian attacks
   d. wanted to defend national honor

2.35 It was the 50th anniversary of the Declaration of Independence.

2.36 He formed an anti-American Confederacy among Indians all over the eastern Mississippi.

2.37 Any order:
   a. small navy
   b. small, disorganized army

c. militia would not leave the country

d. no National Bank

e. very little income from tariffs

or: new taxes not raised before the war

2.38 mainly from the west, some from the south

2.39 They found British guns and powder in the Indian's camp.

2.40 They had not fought in the Revolution and had no memory of the difficulties of war.

2.41 Canada

2.42 He said he had ended his trade restrictions when he had not. Madison believed him and restarted the embargo against Britain.

2.43 June 1812

2.44 Any order:

a. impressment

b. seizure of U.S. ships and cargoes

c. aid to Indians

SECTION THREE

3.1 g

3.2 f

3.3 c

3.4 b

3.5 e

3.6 h

3.7 i

3.8 a

3.9 d

3.10 Mr. Madison's War

3.11 Michilimackinac

3.12 Old Ironsides

3.13 "We have met the enemy and they are ours."

3.14 privateers

3.15 Any order:

a. They opposed Napoleon and did not want to help defeat Britain.

b. The war cut off all trade with Britain.

3.16 Canada

3.17 The frigates were larger, with better guns. All of the American ships were manned by free patriots, not men forced into the job.

3.18 He built five ships on Lake Erie and had five more towed up the Niagara River by oxen.

3.19 Napoleon was defeated in Europe.

3.20 An Indian nation south of the Great Lakes, British control of the Lakes and British keep land in Maine.

3.21 They did not get the victories they expected.

3.22 To inflict several defeats on America and then make demands for land in exchange for peace.

3.23 A hastily assembled militia force.

3.24 John Quincy Adams

3.25 Maine

3.26 They blockaded the American coast; doubled up their ships–no more single sailing

3.27 Battle of Plattsburg Bay, Thomas Macdonough

3.28 Burned most of the public buildings.

3.29 by land and sea

3.30 Fort McHenry

3.31 Lundy's Lane and Chippewa

3.32 A return to the status quo

3.33 Teacher check. This is an example:

Can you see when the sun rises or what we saw last evening? The flag that was flying over the fortifications through the dangerous night. The light from the bombs and rockets showed it was still there. Does that star-studded flag still wave over the land of the free and brave?

Thus it will always be when free men protect the homes they love from the ravages of war. Blessed with both peace and victory, may the land God rescued praise Him who made and preserved our nation. We will win when we fight for a just cause under the motto, "In God is our trust." Does that star-studded flag and still wave over the land of the free and brave?

3.34 Andrew Jackson

3.35 Hartford Convention

3.36 Creek

3.37 two weeks

3.38 Florida

3.39 Horseshoe Bend

3.40 Andrew Jackson, Seminole

3.41 Adams-Onis

3.42 manufacturing

3.43 arbitration

3.44 respect

3.45 They began to steadily improve. They did not fight any more wars, but settled problems by diplomacy.

3.46 The war had removed the major Indian and foreign power menace there.

3.47 They made a frontal attack on a well-fortified position.

3.48 That America won the war.

3.49 To expand across the continent.

3.50 Any order:
   a. tariff to protect industry
   b. National Bank
   c. improve transportation

3.51 a. 640
   b. 320
   c. 160
   d. 80

3.52 Era of Good Feelings

3.53 a. *Dartmouth College v. Woodard*
   b. *Culloch v. Maryland*
   c. *Gibbons v. Ogden*
   d. *Fletcher v. Peck*
   e. *Cohens v. Virginia*

3.54 Any order:
   a. America closed to more European colonies
   b. any European intervention in the Americas would be viewed as a hostile act against the U.S.
   c. U.S. would not intervene in Europe
   d. U.S. would not interfere with current European Colonies

3.55 Nationalism

3.56 Improvements within a state were opposed because they believed it was unconstitutional to use federal money for a project in just one state.

3.57 a. Nicholas Biddle
   b. Panic of 1819

3.58 Eastern Mississippi

3.59 Great Britain

3.60 a. John Marshall
   b. Hamilton's Federalists

3.61 Its tighter policies contributed to the Panic of 1819 and it foreclosed on many farms, especially in the west.

3.62 a. Cumberland Road
   b. 1811
   c. Cumberland, Maryland to Vandalia, Illinois

3.63 turnpikes

SECTION ONE

1.1	d	1.31	
1.2	a,d	1.32	✔
1.3	b	1.33	"Jackson and Reform."
1.4	c	1.34	Tariff of Abominations
1.5	a	1.35	Andrew Jackson
1.6	a	1.36	Old Man Eloquent
1.7	d	1.37	A series of resolutions that barred any petition on slavery from being heard in the House.
1.8	b		
1.9	a,d		
1.10	a	1.38	Henry Clay
1.11	d	1.39	adultery and bigamy
1.12	c	1.40	a
1.13	d	1.41	b
1.14	a	1.42	c
1.15	b	1.43	d
1.16	Any order:	1.44	e
	a. slavery	1.45	d
	b. tariff	1.46	a
1.17	Any order:	1.47	f
	a. Missouri admitted as slave state	1.48	f
	b. Maine admitted as free state	1.49	c
	c. no slavery north of 36° 30′ in the Louisiana Purchase	1.50	a
		1.51	d
1.18	cotton gin	1.52	e
1.19		1.53	e
1.20		1.54	b
1.21	✔	1.55	d
1.22		1.56	c
1.23	✔	1.57	d
1.24		1.58	He was slashed with a sword across the face and hand for refusing to clean a British officer's boots.
1.25	✔		
1.26	✔		
1.27	✔		
1.28		1.59	duels
1.29	✔		
1.30	✔		

1.60 Any order:
    a. hatred of Indians
    b. distrust of banks
    c. determination to expand the nation

1.61 A state can nullify any federal law they believed was unconstitutional.

1.62 kitchen cabinet

1.63 John Calhoun

1.64 Martin Van Buren

1.65 He hoped to hurt Jackson's popularity in the election of 1832 by forcing him to charter a bank distrusted by the west or veto it when eastern businessmen wanted it.

1.66 Andrew Jackson

1.67 Trail of Tears

1.68 pet

1.69 tariff

1.70 Panic of 1837

1.71 censure

1.72 speculation

1.73 Seminole

1.74 Cherokee

1.75 Force

1.76 hang

1.77 Black Hawk

1.78 Martin Van Buren

1.79 Jackson

1.80 Martin Van Buren

1.81 A new tariff was passed that gradually reduced the tariff over a number of years.

1.82 That the Indians would be moved to lands where they would be forever free from white encroachment.

1.83 He moved federal money out of it and placed it into loyal state banks.

SECTION TWO

2.1 g

2.2 f

2.3 d

2.4 c

2.5 a

2.6 b

2.7 Log cabin; Hard Cider

2.8 Henry Clay

2.9 Democratic

2.10 Webster-Ashburton

2.11 Oregon Trail

2.12 Columbia River; 49th parallel

2.13 harbor

2.14 "Fifty-four Forty or Fight."

2.15 "Tippecanoe and Tyler, too."

2.16 His Accidency

2.17 Aroostook

2.18 American Desert

2.19 49th

2.20 Any order: a national bank, higher tariffs, internal improvements

2.21 Texas; Oregon

2.22 Marcus Whitman

2.23 Britain

2.24 2,000

2.25 false; change *Moses* to *Stephen*

2.26 false; change *Most* to *All*

2.27 true

2.28 false; change *Goliad* to *San Jacinto*

2.29 true

2.30 true

2.31 false; change *Webster-Ashburton* to *Adams-Onis*

2.32 false; change *Henry Clay* to *James Polk*

2.33 true

2.34 true

2.35 Any order: William Travis, Jim Bowie, Davy Crockett

2.36 Any order:
  a. lower the tariff
  b. create an independent treasury
  c. settle border dispute in Oregon
  d. add California to the U.S.

2.37 Gone to Texas

2.38 He sent Zachary Taylor into an area of South Texas claimed by Mexico hoping the Mexicans would attack and they did.

2.39 Santa Anna declared himself dictator and suspended the constitution.

2.40 "Remember the Alamo! Remember Goliad!"

2.41 He retreated in front of Santa Anna, gaining strength as Santa Anna lost his.

2.42 b

2.43 a

2.44 b

2.45 c

2.46 a

2.47 d

2.48 e

2.49 f

2.50 b

2.51 b

2.52 c

2.53 g

2.54 b

2.55 f

2.56 the Military Academy at West Point

2.57 Civil War

2.58 It was questionable whether it began with an attack on American soil. It was believed to be a conspiracy to add slave states. It was feared that fighting over the new territory might divide the nation.

2.59 He believed they were politically motivated.

2.60 artillery

2.61 Guadalupe-Hidalgo

2.62 slavery

2.63 Old Fuss and Feathers

2.64 gold

2.65 Zachary Taylor

2.66 Free Soil

2.67 Gadsden

2.68 Forty-niners

2.69 Mexico City

2.70 Nicholas Trist

2.71 Any order:
  a. overland via wagon trail
  b. by ship to the Isthmus of Panama, across, and north again by ship
  c. around South America by ship

2.72 fifteen million

2.73 Santa Anna

2.74 1849; territory

2.75 "Free soil, free speech, free labor, free men."

2.76 railroad

2.77 Cerro Gordo

2.78 Mexican Cession

2.79 Rio Grande

2.80 Wilmont

2.81 slavery

2.82 Millard Fillmore

2.83 Winfield Scott

SECTION THREE

3.1   h

3.2   e

3.3   e

3.4   g

3.5   h

3.6   d

3.7   c

3.8   f

3.9   g

3.10   a

3.11   h

3.12   b

3.13   Britain

3.14   it became profitable

3.15   Any three: water source, capital, population, poor soil, seaports

3.16   Any four: long hours, low wages, use of children, unsafe working conditions, no job protection, law opposed unions

3.17   A change from farming and hand crafts to industry and machine manufacturing.

3.18   Cities devoted to manufacturing needed transport to get food from the farms and a way to ship finished goods.

3.19   There was a strong feeling against using federal money to benefit one state.

3.20   It connected the west with the cities of the east even when the Mississippi River was in Confederate hands.

3.21   States saw the success of the Erie Canal and wanted to copy it.

3.22   steamships

3.23   a

3.24   c

3.25   a

3.26   h

3.27   d

3.28   f

3.29   g

3.30   g

3.31   b

3.32   f

3.33   b

3.34   a

3.35   h

3.36   c

3.37   f

3.38   e

3.39   e

3.40   d

3.41   d

3.42   Second Great Awakening

3.43   Know-Nothing

3.44   Any order: Ireland; Germany

3.45   polygamy

3.46   Potato Famine

3.47   camp meetings

3.48   Seneca Falls Convention

3.49   Unitarians

3.50   *The Liberator*

3.51   Temperance

3.52   Joseph Smith

3.53   William Wilberforce

3.54   Any order: Baptists; Methodists

3.55   Brigham Young; Utah

3.56   Any six: prisons, treatment of the insane, debt law, drinking, working conditions, punishments, women's rights, slavery

3.57 true

3.58 true

3.59 false

3.60 true

3.61 false

3.62 false

3.63 true

3.64 false

3.65 false

3.66 true

3.67 Any order:

    a. California admitted as free state

    b. Popular sovereignty in Mexican Cession

    c. Texas border set as it is today

    d. Texas given $10 million compensation

    e. Slave trade ended in Washington D.C.

    f. Fugitive Slave Law

3.68 Clay: proposed and supported it

    Calhoun: opposed it

    Webster: supported it

3.69 Taylor opposed the Compromise, but Fillmore supported it and signed it.

3.70 It had a slave-run plantation economy.

3.71 He used threats and tact to convince Japan to allow trade with the U.S.

3.72 A plan to take Cuba by force if Spain refused to sell. It embarrassed Pierce's administration and caused him to back away from Cuba.

3.73 A series of people and homes that hid and helped runaway slaves reach Canada.

3.74

3.75

3.76 ✔

3.77 ✔

3.78 ✔

3.79

3.80 ✔

3.81 ✔

3.82

3.83 *Uncle Tom's Cabin*

3.84 Stephen Douglas

3.85 Republican

3.86 Harriet Beecher Stowe

3.87 northern

3.88 K

3.89

3.90 K

3.91 K

3.92

3.93

3.94 K

3.95

3.96

SECTION ONE

1.1   Brooks; Sumner

1.2   Any order: James Buchanan, John Frémont, Millard Fillmore

1.3   Democratic

1.4   James Buchanan; Stephen Douglas

1.5   1830s

1.6   agriculture

1.7   south

1.8   Lawrence

1.9   anti-

1.10 The Crime Against Kansas

1.11 John Brown

1.12 Free soil, free men, and Frémont

1.13 The abolitionist movement along with the north's larger population, political power, and the growth of the anti-slavery Republican Party.

1.14 They ignored it as much as possible.

1.15 It protected slavery. The people could vote for the constitution only, with or without slavery. Thus, the anti-slavery voters could not stop slavery by voting against it.

1.16 The pro and anti-slavery factions fought with each other.

1.17 He had been in Britain and had not been involved with the unpopular Kansas-Nebraska Act.

1.18 He had lived in free states for several years.

1.19 The arsenal at Harper's Ferry

1.20 Robert E. Lee

1.21 speculation in land and railroads

1.22 Lincoln-Douglas Debates

1.23 That Scott could not sue because he was not a citizen.

1.24 That he was property that was fully protected by the Constitution from seizure.

1.25 Slavery could only safely exist in a state if the local governments passed laws to protect it.

1.26 He was tried and hanged.

1.27 Any order:
      a. Abraham Lincoln–Republican
      b. Stephen Douglas–Democrat (north)
      c. John Breckinridge–Democrat (south)
      d. John Bell–Constitutional Union

1.28 Slavery was legal in all of the U.S.

1.29 It was morally wrong. It could not be ended where it already existed, but it must not spread.

1.30 He became an abolitionist martyr.

1.31 Any order:
      a. no expansion of slavery
      b. protective tariff
      c. internal improvements
      d. transcontinental railroad in north
      e. protect rights of immigrants

1.32 a. The north refused to accept it and the south applauded it.
      b. The south had little trouble with it and saw themselves as superior as a result.
      c. The south saw the public support of Brown's violence as a threat.

1.33 Fort Sumter

1.34 Abraham Lincoln

1.35 4

1.36 Crittenden

1.37 James Buchanan

1.38 Any order: Missouri, Kentucky, Delaware, Maryland

1.39 Honest Abe

1.40 South Carolina

1.41 Any order:
  a. called for volunteers
  b. suspended civil rights in border areas
  c. ordered blockade of southern ports
  d. ordered federal money to pay for the war effort

1.42 House of Representatives

1.43 provisions

1.44 Jefferson Davis

1.45 Montgomery, Alabama; Richmond, Virginia

1.46 West Virginia; 1863

1.47 S

1.48 N

1.49 N

1.50 S

1.51 S

1.52 N

1.53 N

1.54 S

1.55 N

1.56 N

1.57 S

1.58 N

1.59 N

1.60 It cut off incoming trade and stopped outgoing cotton which was the major source of southern income, creating shortages of money and supplies.

1.61 They did not favor the American democratic experiment, the south had a European-like aristocratic culture, and Confederacy would be an advantageous trading partner.

1.62 Corn, wheat, and the purchase of war material

1.63 An American warship arrested two Confederate diplomats on a British steamer. Britain threatened war. The men were released and their capture disavowed.

1.64 Emancipation Proclamation

SECTION TWO

2.1 Military tactics used mass attacks from the days when weapons were inaccurate and slow. The faster, more accurate Civil War weapons made such attacks slaughters.

2.2 He rebuilt, organized, and supplied a large, effective Union army.

2.3 He was hesitant to attack unless he was certain of superior numbers and position.

2.4 World War II

2.5 620,000

2.6 First Bull Run

2.7 Donelson

2.8 New Orleans

2.9 First Bull Run

2.10 First Bull Run

2.11 Fort Henry

2.12 Shiloh

2.13 First Bull Run

2.14 Henry and Donelson

2.15 Shiloh

2.16   Corinth

2.17   First Bull Run

2.18   First Bull Run

2.19   Emancipation Proclamation

2.20   Fair Oaks (Seven Pines)

2.21   *Monitor*

2.22   Seven Days

2.23   Antietam

2.24   Second Bull Run

2.25   Robert E. Lee

2.26   Antietam

2.27   Fredricksburg

2.28   Stonewall Jackson

2.29   Emancipation Proclamation

2.30   *Merrimac*

2.31   British West Indies

2.32   Fair Oaks (Seven Pines)

2.33   Seven Days

2.34   Antietam

2.35   Fredricksburg

2.36   McClellan

2.37   Gettysburg

2.38   Chancellorsville

2.39   Vicksburg

2.40   Murfreesboro

2.41   Vicksburg

2.42   Chancellorsville

2.43   Gettysburg

2.44   Gettysburg

2.45   Vicksburg

2.46   Gettysburg

2.47   Gettysburg

2.48   Chancellorsville

2.49   Chancellorsville

2.50   Gettysburg

2.51   eighty-seven years

2.52   It had already been dedicated by the men who had fought and died there. They could not add to that dedication.

2.53   to finishing the work (the war) those men had died for

2.54   these dead shall not have died in vain

2.55   He failed to pursue Lee who was allowed to escape.

2.56   William Rosencrans; Braxton Bragg

2.57   Confederate

2.58   200,000–300,000

2.59   George Thomas

2.60   Andersonville

2.61   Sanitary Commission

2.62   Any order: paying a substitute; paying a $300 fee

2.63   Union

2.64   Chickamauga

2.65   Rock of

2.66   Battle above the Clouds

2.67   Ulysses S. Grant

2.68   amputation

2.69   the draft law

2.70   Chattanooga

2.71   Petersburg

2.72   Jubal Early

2.73   Cold Harbor

2.74   Wilderness

2.75   David Farragut

2.76   George McClellan

2.77   Andrew Johnson

2.78   William T. Sherman

2.79   Copperheads

2.80   Philip Sheridan

2.81   Mobile, Alabama

2.82   War Democrats

2.83   John Hood

2.84 lieutenant-general

2.85 When his army was mauled by Lee, he kept going.

2.86 The re-election of Abraham Lincoln

2.87 Attack, shift, attack, and keep at it until Lee gave out

2.88 Everything that might aid the enemy is destroyed. (farms, factories, crops, etc.)

2.89 false; change *Nashville* to *Atlanta*

2.90 true

2.91 false; change *January* to *April*

2.92 true

2.93 true

2.94 false; change *Richmond* to *Appomattox Courthouse*

2.95 false; change *Grant* to *Sheridan*

2.96 true

2.97 true

2.98 false; change *was captured* to *fled*

2.99 true

2.100 true

2.101 false; change *rifles* to *horses*

2.102 false; change *hanged after a trial* to *shot by Union troops*

2.103 true

2.104 false; change *Meade* to *Grant*

2.015 Teacher check

SECTION THREE

3.1 ten percent

3.2 Any order:
    a. approve the 13th Amendment
    b. repudiate Confederate debts
    c. repeal secession

3.3 Radical Republicans

3.4 Thirteenth

3.5 tailor

3.6 Civil Rights Act

3.7 Freedmen's Bureau

3.8 overrode it

3.9 Any order:
    a. made Freedmen citizens
    b. cut Congressional representation if they were denied the right to vote
    c. barred certain Confederate leaders from office
    d. voided Confederate debts

3.10 He hoped to influence Congressional elections to get a body that favored his reconstruction plan.

3.11 He believed it interfered with the rights of southern states.

3.12 Any order:
    a. Homestead Act
    b. high tariff
    c. subsidy for northern transcontinental railroad

3.13 To keep the blacks subjugated and as a cheap labor supply for the south.

3.14 Tennessee

3.15 National Union Party

3.16 He did not secede with his state.

3.17 Joint Committee on Reconstruction

3.18 Thaddeus Stevens

3.19 carpetbaggers

3.20 5

3.21 Seward's Folly or Icebox

3.22 share crop

3.23 Ku Klux Klan

3.24 Fifteenth

3.25 Seven

3.26 Ulysses S. Grant

3.27 7.2 million

3.28 Tenure of Office

3.29 Democratic

3.30 Scalawags

3.31 redeemed

3.32 Edwin Stanton

3.33 Any order:

   a. terrorized blacks who voted

   b. literacy tests

   c. grandfather clauses

3.34 Any order:

   a. corruption

   b. tired of trying to control the south

   c. thought whites should control the government

3.35 They terrorized Republicans, blacks, and others who supported Republican governments

3.36 Any order:

   a. set up public schools

   b. internal improvements

   c. modernized the tax system

3.37 a. Indebted landowners needed cash.

   b. It exhausted the soil.

3.38 They were separated from whites and supplied with less money.

3.39 The president could not successfully be thrown out of office for political reasons.

3.40 hard money

3.41 Horatio Seymour

3.42 Boss Tweed

3.43 Crédit Mobilier

3.44 Resumption Act

3.45 Whiskey Ring

3.46 Greenbacks

3.47 Treaty of Washington

3.48 civil service reform

3.49 Black Friday

3.50 Liberal Republicans

3.51 William Belknap

3.52 $15.5 million

3.53 Thomas Nast

3.54 false

3.55 true

3.56 false

3.57 false

3.58 true

3.59 false

3.60 true

3.61 Democrats and Republicans had different election results in four states.

3.62 He supported civil service reform and appointed men based on ability, not party loyalty.

3.63 secession and slavery

3.64 Hayes was awarded the election. In exchange, he agreed to withdraw the last occupation troops in the south and support a southern continental railroad.

3.65 When Hayes removed the federal troops on occupation duty in 1877.

3.66 The Republicans had 8 of the 15 votes on the committee making the decision.

3.67 She had a college degree, was active in social causes, and banned alcohol in the White House.

3.68 Samuel Tilden; governor of New York, helped put Boss Tweed in jail

3.69 none

3.70 U.S. Representative, governor of Ohio, Union veteran, honest and competent

SECTION ONE

1.1	stockholders	1.28	banned paupers, criminals, contract workers, anarchists, insane, polygamists, those with contagious diseases, and later the illiterate
1.2	Union Pacific, Central Pacific		
1.3	air brakes		
1.4	Pullman sleeping cars and dining cars		
1.5	Andrew Carnegie	1.29	f
1.6	Standard Oil, John D. Rockefeller	1.30	b
1.7	dividends	1.31	e
1.8	created a national market	1.32	c
1.9	took stock from several companies and ran them together	1.33	g
		1.34	a
1.10	a big, industry dominating corporation	1.35	d
1.11	Promontory Point, Utah; May 1869	1.36	c
1.12	They charged more for short hauls, which had no competition, than for long hauls that did. They gave rebates to big customers and divided up business using pools.	1.37	g
		1.38	f
		1.39	e
		1.40	d
		1.41	b
1.13	Bessemer	1.42	a
1.14	holding company	1.43	Any five: typewriter, cash register, adding machine, telephone, electric street cars, refrigeration, improved canning, Kodak camera
1.15	New Immigration		
1.16	Samuel Gompers		
1.17	depression (panic)		
1.18	five million	1.44	Any three: phonograph, light bulb, storage battery, duplicating machine
1.19	Terrence Powderly		
1.20	Chinese	1.45	Any three: typewriter, stock ticker, motion pictures, electric generator, electric trains
1.21	strikes, Gould railroad		
1.22	city political machine		
1.23	Haymarket Riot	1.46	Any order:
1.24	literacy test		a. laissez-faire
1.25	They looked different, kept their old ways, took low paying jobs, and were often non-Protestant.		b. Social Darwinism
			c. admiration for the rich and successful
1.26	It organized a federation of craft unions, not all jobs in one union, and concentrated on job issues.	1.47	Chief Joseph
		1.48	miners
		1.49	*A Century of Dishonor*
1.27	Their strikes halted commerce, were often violent, and unions had small numbers of active members who were anti-capitalism	1.50	160; 5
		1.51	cowboy
		1.52	Sioux
		1.53	Any order: Chisolm, Goodnight-Loving
		1.54	drop; over-grazing

1.55	Grange	1.58	winter of 1886-87
1.56	Any order:	1.59	1890
	a. repeating rifles	1.60	Colonel George Custer
	b. railroad	1.61	Dawes
	c. extermination of buffalo	1.62	Any order: wheat, corn
	d. European diseases	1.63	debt; railroad
1.57	Geronimo	1.64	Any order: railroad, Homestead Act

SECTION TWO

2.1	e
2.2	d
2.3	e
2.4	a
2.5	e
2.6	g
2.7	e
2.8	b
2.9	c
2.10	e
2.11	c
2.12	e
2.13	d
2.14	b
2.15	c
2.16	b
2.17	f
2.18	a
2.19	d
2.20	c
2.21	e
2.22	e
2.23	a
2.24	e
2.25	e
2.26	Mugwumps
2.27	none
2.28	Silver prices had dropped making the

	silver dollar less valuable than a gold one.
2.29	West and South
2.30	The treasury had to buy silver and mint it at a 16 to 1 ratio with gold.
2.31	Pendleton Act
2.32	10 percent
2.33	assassination of President Garfield
2.34	rate discrimination, rebates, pools, charging more for short hauls
2.35	Billion Dollar Congress
2.36	Democrat–Grover Cleveland Republican–Benjamin Harrison
2.37	Democrat–Grover Cleveland Republican–Benjamin Harrison Populist–James Weaver
2.38	Any order: Sherman Silver Purchase Act; McKinley Tariff
2.39	Farmer's Alliance
2.40	depression in 1893
2.41	the tariff
2.42	Sherman Anti-Trust Act
2.43	People's (Populist) Party
2.44	Sherman Silver Purchase Act
2.45	Pullman
2.46	William Jennings Bryan
2.47	Grover Cleveland
2.48	G.A.R. (Civil War veterans)

2.49   silver coinage

2.50   Wilson-Gorman Bill

2.51   selling bonds through J.P. Morgan

2.52   debt, low agriculture prices, railroads

2.53   Eugene Debs

2.54   strikes for better wages

2.55   the courts and government quickly aided the corporation owners

2.56   spent it

2.57   Any order:

   a.   free coinage of silver

   b.   new banking system

   c.   income tax

   d.   government ownership of railroads, telegraph, and telephone

   e.   eight hour day

   f.   restrict immigration

   g.   direct election of senators

2.58   Gold Standard Act

2.59   *Cross of Gold*

2.60   silver coinage

2.61   William J. Bryan

2.62   Marcus Hanna

2.63   A full dinner pail

2.64   William J. Bryan

2.65   Dingley

2.66   William J. Bryan

2.67   William J. Bryan

2.68   Marcus Hanna

2.69   front porch

2.70   fifty cents

2.71   1897

2.72   e

2.73   c

2.74   h

2.75   f

2.76   d

2.77   i

2.78   a

2.79   b

2.80   g

2.81   yellow journalism

2.82   *Maine*

2.83   Open Door

2.84   Teller Amendment

2.85   Philippines

2.86   Spanish-American War

2.87   Rough Riders

2.88   Anti-Imperialist League

2.89   Hawaii

2.90   Boxer Rebellion

2.91   yellow fever

2.92   Platt Amendment

2.93   Kettle or San Juan

2.94   Puerto Rico

2.95   four months

2.96   Santiago

SECTION THREE

3.1   muckrakers

3.2   city

3.3   Wisconsin

3.4   Elkins Act

3.5   Northern Securities Company

3.6   Teddy Bear

3.7   Ira Tarbell

3.8   Full dinner pail

3.9   Square Deal

3.10   Hepburn Act

3.11   Robert La Follette

3.12   Samuel Jones

3.13   Depression of 1893

3.14   Any order: Anti-Saloon League; Women's Christian Temperance Union

3.15   They wanted to use his popularity, but keep him out of power.

3.16   Any eight: secret ballot, primary elections, voter referendums, recall elections, tax reform, regulatory commissions, control of public utilities, civil service reform, open bidding for public contracts, professional city management as well as laws against corruption, prostitution, and unsafe housing

3.17   He revitalized it and made the president the national leader even in legislation.

3.18   Newlands

3.19   Alton Parker

3.20   *The Jungle*; Upton Sinclair

3.21   Colombia

3.22   Big Stick

3.23   Russo-Japanese War

3.24   Moroccan

3.25   1907

3.26   Commerce and Labor

3.27   Roosevelt Corollary

3.28   Port Arthur

3.29   Great White Fleet

3.30   George Goethals

3.31 $400 million; 1914

3.32   segregate Japanese children

3.33   Santo Domingo

3.34   Venezuela

3.35   William Gorgas

3.36   Meat Inspection

3.37   Pure Food and Drug

3.38   He offered to arbitrate and threatened to use the army to mine coal when the owners refused.

3.39   TR supported a revolution in Panama and signed a treaty with the new government.

3.40   The school board reversed the segregation order and Japan limited emigration to the U.S.

3.41   Taft

3.42   Roosevelt

3.43   Wilson

3.44   Bryan

3.45   Roosevelt

3.46   Orville and Wilbur Wright

3.47   Taft

3.48   Robert La Follette

3.49   Joseph Cannon

3.50   Henry Ford

3.51   Taft

3.52   Taft

3.53   Taft

3.54   Henry Ford

3.55   Richard Ballinger

3.56   Taft

3.57   Roosevelt

3.58   Gifford Pinchot

3.59   Any order:
      a. Payne-Aldrich Tariff
      b. Pinchot-Ballinger fight
      c. failed to support move against the power of Joseph Cannon

3.60   to use investment to spread U.S. influence abroad

3.61   Any four:
      a. women's suffrage
      b. minimum wage
      c. government pensions
      d. unemployment compensation; or control of stock market

3.62   He started almost twice as many suits as TR. Standard Oil and the American Tobacco Company were dissolved when he was president.

3.63 Victoriano Huerta

3.64 John Pershing; Pancho Villa

3.65 World War I

3.66 Clayton

3.67 Thomas Jefferson

3.68 Federal Trade

3.69 Any order: tariff reduction, banking reform, anti-trust laws

3.70 Underwood Tariff

3.71 Federal Reserve Board

3.72 Any order: Nicaragua, Haiti, Santo Domingo

3.73 William J. Bryan

3.74 New Jersey; Princeton

3.75 Any order: Roosevelt, Taft, Wilson

3.76 Tampico; Any order: Argentina, Brazil, Chile

SECTION ONE

1.1 Wilhelm II
1.2 Balkan Peninsula
1.3 France
1.4 poison gas
1.5 Archduke Ferdinand
1.6 1st Battle of the Marne
1.7 ace
1.8 Sir Edward Grey
1.9 Alsace, Lorraine
1.10 Otto von Bismarck
1.11 Belgium
1.12 Dardenelles
1.13 zeppelins
1.14 No Man's Land
1.15 Eddie Rickenbacker
1.16 Balance of Power
1.17 a. Sarajevo, Bosnia
  b. Austria-Hungary; Serbia
  c. Austria-Hungary; Serbia
  d. Russia
  e. Germany; Russia; France
  f. Germany; Belgium
  g. Britain; Germany
1.18 To attack and defeat France before Russia could get its huge army into battle
1.19 Alliances, national pride, and an arms race
1.20 The men charged across open ground into established fortifications protected by machine guns and artillery.
1.21 It offered Mexico an alliance with Germany in exchange for recovering the American southwest after a Central Powers victory.
1.22 They attacked without warning, destroyed the ships instead of seizing the cargo and often killed the crew.
1.23 The invasion of neutral Belgium
1.24 Stay neutral at all cost

1.25 "He Kept Us Out of War." It was ironic because he asked Congress to declare war a few months after the election.
1.26 The British had an effective blockade against the Central Powers who could not get loans to buy supplies.
1.27 Neutrality
1.28 It was sunk by a U-boat and 1,198 people died. Bryan resigned rather than sign a strong note of protest.
1.29 A revolution established a democratic government.
1.30 German submarine attacks
1.31 Lenin; communists (Bolsheviks)
1.32 American Expeditionary Force; John Pershing
1.33 influenza
1.34 the world safe for democracy
1.35 War Industries Board
1.36 Doughboys; early 1918
1.37 Château-Thierry; Belleau
1.38 Alvin York
1.39 Herbert Hoover
1.40 Meuse-Argonne
1.41 November 11, 1918; 11:00 A.M.
1.42 Men between 18 and 45 must register. No one could buy an exemption, but some were given to workers in key industries.
1.43 The communists took Russia out of the war, giving Germany a large chunk of east Europe and leaving them free to concentrate on the west.
1.44 America was repaying a debt it owed the America Revolutionary hero from France by defending his nation.
1.45 He wanted them to have control of a section of the front.
1.46 a

1.47 i

1.48 e

1.49 b

1.50 d

1.51 g

1.52 c

1.53 j

1.54 f

1.55 k

1.56 h

1.57 ✔

1.58

1.59

1.60 ✔

1.61 ✔

1.62

1.63

1.64 ✔

1.65

1.66

1.67

1.68 ✔

1.69 ✔

1.70 a. He went on a speaking tour to win the support of the American people.
      b. He collapsed and suffered a stroke.

1.71 It forced Germany to pay large war damages, ruined their economy, created bitterness which led to the rise of Adolf Hitler.

1.72 To make Germany pay for the costs of the war and cripple it so it could never threaten France again.

1.73 They signed a separate peace treaty.

1.74 It included only one minor Republican and no senators.

1.75 The League of Nations

1.76 U.S., Britain, France and Italy

1.77 Territory (the spoils of war)

1.78 the Saar region

1.79 Much of its richest land had been taken from it

1.80 It began to decline.

SECTION TWO

2.1 e

2.2 i

2.3 j

2.4 f

2.5 a

2.6 d

2.7 c

2.8 l

2.9 h

2.10 g

2.11 b

2.12 k

2.13 selling supplies at cut rates; awarding construction contracts

2.14 police strike

2.15 blindly trusted his friends

2.16 Keep Cool with Coolidge

2.17 Treaty of Versailles

2.18 1920; Nineteenth

2.19 quotas; Northern Europe

2.20 Harry M. Daugherty

2.21 a. They should be repaid with interest.
      b. Some should be forgiven as part of the American contribution to the war.

2.22 oil leases

2.23 b

2.24 h

2.25 g

2.26 d

2.27 c

2.28 f

2.29 e

2.30 a

2.31 A time when the sale of alcohol was illegal, 1919-1932

2.32 No. People just drank illegally.

2.33 They began to spend rather than save and used credit to increase their buying power.

2.34 A private saloon during Prohibition.

2.35 A free living woman of the 1920s who drank, smoked, danced, dressed daringly and enjoyed life.

2.36 Any three: illegal drinking, flappers, baseball, boxing, personal sports, movies, crossword puzzles, flagpole sitting, dance marathons

2.37 The rise of organized crime

2.38 A person who does not believe in miracles and sees Christianity as a set of ethics not a relationship with Jesus Christ.

2.39 Fundamentalists

2.40 The public believed Fundamentalists were bigoted fools who didn't accept science.

2.41 Any three: cars, refrigerators, radios, vacuum cleaners, electricity

2.42 Roaring Twenties

2.43 Stock market crash of 1929

2.44 agriculture

2.45 a New Deal

2.46 He provided money to buy surpluses and raised tariffs on food.

2.47 mining engineer

2.48 Take a loan to buy stock and use the stock itself as collateral for the loan.

2.49 Hawley-Smoot tariff

2.50 They wanted early payment of a bonus promised to World War I veterans.

They were chased out of Washington by the army.

2.51 After the crash people cut their spending as a precaution. Businesses cut back production, employment and wages as purchases fell. That meant people had even less money to spend and made fewer purchases.

2.52 ✔

2.53 ✔

2.54

2.55 ✔

2.56 ✔

2.57 ✔

2.58

2.59 ✔

2.60 ✔

2.61 ✔

2.62

2.63 He immediately declared a bank holiday, promising that only safe banks would reopen.

2.64 F.D.R. wanted to add a new justice for every one over 70 years old because the court was throwing out New Deal laws.

2.65 Any two: It increased the size and expense of the government, increased government regulation and set up the regular use of deficit spending.

2.66 Good Neighbor Policy

2.67 His legs were paralyzed and his character strengthened.

2.68 k

2.69 h

2.70 l

2.71 i

2.72 c

2.73 o

2.74 n

2.75	d	2.80	b
2.76	m	2.81	e
2.77	j	2.82	f
2.78	a	2.83	1929; stock market; 1933; 25; New Deal; 1937; 1938; 1942; World War II
2.79	g		

SECTION THREE

3.1 appeasement

3.2 Miracle at Dunkirk

3.3 Maginot Line

3.4 Benito Mussolini

3.5 Berlin-Rome-Tokyo Axis

3.6 Phony War

3.7 Sudentenland

3.8 Neville Chamberlain

3.9 blitzkrieg

3.10 Battle of Britain

3.11 Spanish Civil War

3.12 Adolf Hitler

3.13 Any order: Denmark, Norway

3.14 Neutrality Acts

3.15 Winston Churchill

3.16 Any order: Belgium, Netherlands

3.17 Vichy France

3.18 the Blitz

3.19 Poland

3.20 Joseph Stalin

3.21 invasion of Poland

3.22 Francisco Franco

3.23 Manchukuo

3.24 Ethiopia

3.25 sue for peace

3.26 France, seas, oceans, air, beaches, landing grounds, hills, and Empire

3.27 In the same railroad car where Germany signed the armistice in 1918

3.28 Japanese; Pearl Harbor, Hawaii

3.29 Harry S. Truman

3.30 Atlantic

3.31 *U.S.S. Arizona*

3.32 Wendell Willkie; Thomas Dewey

3.33 that will live in infamy

3.34 a. Any order: conscription law, traded destroyers for bases
   b. Lend-lease approved
   c. U.S. navy convoyed merchant ships to Iceland
   d. Any order: U.S. merchant ships armed and carried cargo all the way to Britain

3.35 They destroyed much of the Pacific fleet but they united America against them.

3.36 Japan captured southeast Asia, the main source of natural rubber. It was solved by creating a synthetic rubber industry.

3.37 Any four: unity, rationing, scrap drives, Victory gardens, full employment, massive arms production, consumer goods not available, price/production controls

3.38 They were forced into internment camps in the Midwest.

3.39 c

3.40 e

3.41 f

3.42 g

3.43 h

3.44 i

3.45 h

3.46	b
3.47	f
3.48	e
3.49	d
3.50	a
3.51	b
3.52	c
3.53	d
3.54	d
3.55	e
3.56	a
3.57	e
3.58	d
3.59	e
3.60	c
3.61	i
3.62	b
3.63	h
3.64	e
3.65	g
3.66	h
3.67	g
3.68	a
3.69	c
3.70	d
3.71	g
3.72	d
3.73	c
3.74	g
3.75	Edwin Rommel
3.76	Bernard Montgomery
3.77	Charles de Gaulle
3.78	George Marshall
3.79	George Patton
3.80	Adolf Hitler
3.81	Dwight Eisenhower
3.82	Zhukov
3.83	Admiral Karl Doenitz
3.84	Omar Bradley

3.85	Soviet
3.86	Cairo-Tehran Conferences
3.87	He did not want to come into conflict with the Red Army and he needed to send men south into the Alps.
3.88	the Allies
3.89	Guadalcanal
3.90	Battle of Leyte Gulf
3.91	island hopping
3.92	Midway
3.93	Chester Nimitz
3.94	Doolittle's Raid
3.95	Chiang Kai-shek
3.96	Iwo Jima
3.97	Manhattan Project
3.98	Douglas MacArthur
3.99	Bataan Death March
3.100	Himalaya Mountains
3.101	July 16, 1945
3.102	Battle of Philippine Sea
3.103	kamikaze
3.104	Battle of the Coral Sea
3.105	Potsdam
3.106	Marianas
3.107	Any order: Hiroshima, Nagasaki
3.108	53 million
3.109	Corregidor
3.110	Seabees
3.111	Tarawa
3.112	Okinawa
3.113	Any five: Guam, Wake, Philippines, Hong Kong, Singapore, Indochina, Thailand, Dutch East Indies, Malay Peninsula, most of New Guinea, Burma
3.114	The Japanese defenders would not surrender. Almost all had to be killed in hard fighting.
3.115	They committed suicide.
3.116	two days

SECTION ONE

1.1   Any order: Democracy, communism

1.2   Security Council

1.3   containment

1.4   Berlin Airlift

1.5   NATO

1.6   Truman

1.7   Marshall Plan

1.8   Iron Curtain

1.9   Any order: Turkey, Greece

1.10   United Nations

1.11   Baruch Plan

1.12   It was divided into four parts occupied by the Soviet Union, U.S., Britain and France.

1.13   The Soviet Union refused to allow its section to rejoin the others and set up a communist government there.

1.14   The fall of the Czech Republic to communism

1.15   Any order: Yugoslavia, Bulgaria, Romania, Poland, East Germany, Hungary and Albania, Czechoslovakia

1.16   They refused to remove their troops from Iran until threatened and refused to participate in a plan for international control of nuclear power.

1.17   a. Led by the U.S.–democracies, mainly in Europe
       b. Led by the U.S.S.R.–communist nations
       c. Poorer nations not part of the other two blocks

1.18   Communism would be contained where it already existed by aiding nations threatened by it.

1.19   Teacher check–can include the differences in systems and ideas, Soviet aggression, fear and distrust

1.20   g

1.21   d

1.22   f

1.23   h

1.24   e

1.25   a

1.26   d

1.27   b

1.28   c

1.29   e

1.30   g

1.31   h

1.32   a

1.33   b

1.34   c

1.35   Any order: Soviets set off their first atomic bomb, Communists won the civil war in China

1.36   They were boycotting the council over Taiwan

1.37   Pusan Perimeter

1.38   Austria

1.39   repatriation of prisoners

1.40   fall of the Dien Bien Phu fortress

1.41   The Soviet Union invaded, overthrew the new government and restored communism.

1.42   amphibious landing behind enemy lines at Inchon

1.43   38th Parallel

1.44   Any order: France, Britain, Israel

1.45   Soviet Union occupied the north after World War II while the U.S. occupied the south. Each set up its own kind of government

1.46   Warsaw Pact

1.47   a. The president could use armed force to protect any Middle East nation that asked for help against communism.
       b. Lebanon

1.48	U-2 Affair	1.64	Gulf of Tonkin Resolution
1.49	Berlin Wall	1.65	television
1.50	Cuban Missile Crisis	1.66	Tet Offensive
1.51	Bay of Pigs	1.67	Ngo Dinh Diem
1.52	Sputnik I	1.68	Viet Cong; Vietminh
1.53	NASA	1.69	Vietnamization
1.54	Fulgencio Batista	1.70	Pol Pot; Khmer Rouge
1.55	Fidel Castro	1.71	domino
1.56	ICBM	1.72	destroy the communists; North Vietnam
1.57	U.S.S.R.	1.73	Saigon
1.58	United States	1.74	guerrilla
1.59	Nikita Khrushchev	1.75	re-education; boat people
1.60	Cuba	1.76	cease-fire; withdraw
1.61	Any order: Kennedy, Khrushchev	1.77	protests
1.62	Berlin	1.78	Any order: Laos, Cambodia
1.63	invade Cuba		

SECTION TWO

2.1	Fair Deal	2.22	Thomas Dewey, the Republican, was expected to win because the Democrats were divided. He lost because Truman campaigned hard on specific issues. Dewey did not.
2.2	Joseph McCarthy		
2.3	Booker T. Washington		
2.4	inflation		
2.5	Alger Hiss		
2.6	Dwight Eisenhower	2.23	Any order: civil rights, nationals health insurance, agricultural reform
2.7	Any order: Democrat, Progressive, States' Rights (Dixiecrat)		
		2.24	By the content of their character
2.8	Taft-Hartley	2.25	"My Country 'Tis of Thee"
2.9	Federal Employee Loyalty Program	2.26	Constitution and Declaration of Independence
2.10	I like Ike		
2.11	W.E.B. DuBois	2.27	sit down at a table of brotherhood
2.12	Rosa Parks	2.28	not to use physical violence or resort to wrongful deeds
2.13	Little Rock, Arkansas		
2.14	G.I. Bill of Rights	2.29	Teacher check
2.15	Earl Warren	2.30	Johnson
2.16	Any order: interstate highway system, St. Lawrence Seaway	2.31	Profiles in Courage
		2.32	the New Frontier; Great Society
2.17	Richard Nixon	2.33	televised debates
2.18	*Brown v. Board of Education*	2.34	Vietnam War
2.19	Martin Luther King	2.35	nonviolent
2.20	Julius and Ethel Rosenberg	2.36	Martin Luther King; James Earl Ray
2.21	*Plessy v. Ferguson*	2.37	John Kennedy; Harvey Oswald

2.38 Peace Corps

2.39 legislator

2.40 Alliance for Progress

2.41 "I Have a Dream"

2.42 PT Boat

2.43 attacks on peaceful protesters in Birmingham, Ala.; John Kennedy

2.44 the atmosphere, underwater and outer space; hot line

2.45 sit quietly at the table when they were refused service

2.46 Richard Nixon; Barry Goldwater

2.47 Watts, Los Angeles

2.48 balance of power

2.49 détente

2.50 Nixon Doctrine

2.51 Leonid Brezhnev

2.52 Vietnam

2.53 antiwar protesters

2.54 Richard Nixon

2.55 Watergate

2.56 Stagflation

2.57 Gerald Ford

2.58 Kent State Univ., Ohio

2.59 Busing

2.60 people 18 or older could vote

2.61 "bug" the Democratic headquarters

2.62 Spiro Agnew

2.63 Any order: Archibald Cox, Leon Jawarski

2.64 Taiwan

2.65 Warren Burger

2.66 War Powers Act

2.67 Hubert Humphrey

2.68 George McGovern

2.69 Any order: SALT; an agreement not to increase the number of missiles for five years

2.70 John Dean

2.71 tape recordings of all conversations

2.72 Robert Kennedy

2.73 the youth rebellions of the 1960s

2.74 Henry Kissinger

2.75 marriage, careers, morals, traditions

2.76 He was very anticommunist

2.77 Any two: increased drug use, increased divorce, increased illegitimate children, falling moral standards

2.78 He tried to balance the budget but then tried a price freeze and price controls

2.79 Teacher check

SECTION THREE

3.1 human rights

3.2 invasion of Afghanistan

3.3 OPEC

3.4 Whip Inflation Now (WIN)

3.5 Iran Hostage Crisis

3.6 interest rates

3.7 honest outsider

3.8 *Mayaguez*

3.9 pardoned Nixon

3.10 Panama Canal; Panama

3.11 China

3.12 Camp David Accords

3.13 Nelson Rockefeller

3.14 boycotting; withdrawing

3.15 52; 444

3.16 Ayatollah Khomeini; Mohammad Reza Pahlavi

3.17 Iraq

3.18 Edward Kennedy

3.19 Ronald Reagan

3.20 He hoped to convince Iran to free American hostages in Beruit.

3.21 Weapons were sold to Iran, the profits were sent to the *Contras*, guerrillas who were fighting a pro-communist regime in Nicaragua.

3.22 Any order:
  a. suicide bomb attack on military barracks in Lebanon, 1983
  b. TWA jet hijacked, 1985
  c. *Achille Lauro* hijacked, 1985
  d. bomb in German disco, 1986
  or hostages held in Lebanon

3.23 *perestroika*–restructuring of the economy
  glasnost–openness, greater freedom of speech

3.24 It was an oppressive government supported by the U.S.S.R. and was sending weapons to rebel groups in nearby nations.

3.25 Any order:
  a. reduced taxes
  b. cut welfare
  c. reduced the power of federal regulatory agencies
  d. increased military spending

3.26 The U.S. invaded to overthrow a communist government that was building an airport for a possible Soviet base.

3.27 It was the first treaty to reduce, not just limit nuclear weapons.

3.28 four

3.29 Any three: cost of paying for revolutions all over the world, out-of-date industries, slow to develop computer technology and people worked as little as possible

3.30 inflation

3.31 Sandra Day O'Connor

3.32 Strategic Defense Initiative–space based missile defense system

3.33 air traffic controllers

3.34 e

3.35 c

3.36 f

3.37 b

3.38 h

3.39 d

3.40 g

3.41 a

3.42 Savings and Loan Crisis

3.43 *Exxon Valdez*

3.44 Police officers who had been videotaped beating a black man were acquitted

3.45 1989

3.46 1991

3.47 Persian Gulf War

3.48 Norman Schwarzkopf

3.49 Daniel Noriega

3.50 Colin Powell

3.51 Saddam Hussein

3.52 They shifted their forces north to go into Iraq around the defenses on the border of Kuwait, trapping the Iraqi army.

3.53 U.S.S.R. had held elections that allowed communists to compete for seats, reformers won most of them.

3.54 Coalition missiles and bombs had destroyed all radar and air surveillance.

3.55 fifteen

SECTION ONE

1.1   North Korea, China, Cuba

1.2   Tiananmen Square

1.3   Timothy McVeigh

1.4   Republican

1.5   Somalia

1.6   NAFTA

1.7   Yugoslavia

1.8   Jean-Bertrand Aristide

1.9   Persian Gulf War

1.10 recession

1.11 Contract with America

1.12 Newt Gingrich

1.13 two charges of perjury

1.14 three witnesses testified by video tape

1.15 U.S. prepared to invade but Jimmy Carter convinced the military leaders to leave prior to invasion

1.16 $290 billion

1.17 Ross Perot

1.18 They were sent back to Cuba, not allowed to settle in the U.S.

1.19 He was acquitted, the impeachment did not even get a majority vote

1.20 $5.6 trillion

1.21 g

1.22 i

1.23 h

1.24 a

1.25 d

1.26 j

1.27 f

1.28 c

1.29 b

1.30 e

1.31 c

1.32 d

1.33 e

1.34 a

1.35 b

1.36 divorce

1.37 It is socially acceptable, and selfishness is encouraged by society.

1.38 a. Prison Fellowship
      b. Barney Clark
      c. Focus on the Family
      d. racist propaganda, altered history, and adult content

1.39 euthanasia and abortion

1.40 They can keep the body functioning after the person is dead.

1.41 gathering information, communication, navigation

1.42 a. vacuum tubes
      b. transistors
      c. integrated circuits
      d. microprocessors

1.43 as an interconnection of government and military computers

1.44 Teacher check

1.45 e

1.46 c

1.47 d

1.48 f

1.49 a

1.50 b

1.51 false

1.52 false

1.53 false

1.54 true

1.55 true

1.56 false

SECTION TWO

2.1 Any order:
  a. Crusades
  b. Marco Polo's travels
2.2 a. John Cabot
  b. Francis Drake
  c. London Company
  d. Sir Walter Raleigh
  e. Henry Hudson
2.3 Hudson R. area, Dutch West India Co.
2.4 The Great Lakes, St. Lawrence River, Mississippi River
2.5 Henry the Navigator; around Africa
2.6 Christopher Columbus
2.7 a. Jolliet and Marquette
  b. Jacques Cartier
  c. Samuel de Champlain
  d. La Salle
2.8 Any order:
  a. House of Burgesses established
  b. A shipload of women arrived
  c. 1st African slaves arrived
2.9 Either order:
  a. De Soto
  b. Balboa
  c. Ponce de Leon
  d. Magellan
  e. Coronado
2.10 Either order:
  a. underestimated the distance
  b. did not know America was there
2.11 Patroon
2.12 French
2.13 Jamestown
2.14 the headright
2.15 tobacco
2.16 conquest of wealthy empires (Aztec and Inca)
2.17 Any two:
  European diseases, colonists had better weapons, Indians did not work

together and were overwhelmed by the number of colonists
2.18 furs
2.19 New York
2.20 Massachusetts (Bay)
2.21 Maryland
2.22 Roger Williams
2.23 Royal
2.24 William Penn
2.25 governor, council, assembly
2.26 Mayflower Compact
2.27 company, proprietary, self-governing
2.28 finances
2.29 North Carolina
2.30 New York
2.31 Squanto
2.32 South Carolina
2.33 Rhode Island
2.34 Fundamental Orders of Connecticut
2.35 Thomas Hooker
2.36 Massachusetts (Bay)
2.37 Pennsylvania, Delaware
2.38 Pennsylvania, Delaware, Maryland
2.39 Georgia
2.40 Maine
2.41 settlers didn't pay their rent
2.42 Puritan church members
2.43 George Washington
2.44 Congregationalists
2.45 Great Awakening
2.46 King Philip's War
2.47 New England
2.48 Anglican Church
2.49 Any order: Fishing, whaling, ship building
2.50 New England Confederation
2.51 French and Indian
2.52 Deism
2.53 The south
2.54 William Pitt

2.55 Edward Braddock

2.56 George Whitefield; Jonathan Edwards

2.57 King William's War–War of the League of Augsburg; Queen Anne's War–War of the Spanish Succession; King George's War–War of the Austrian Succession

2.58 Middle colonies

2.59 New England

2.60 Dominion of New England

2.61 Albany Congress

2.62 Middle Colonies

2.63 New England

2.64 Proclamation of 1763

2.65 Any four: Britain was the dominant world power and deeply in debt, colonists began to work together and gained military experience, Britain was angry over the lack of colonial support and unity

2.66 First Continental Congress

2.67 Quebec Act

2.68 Lexington

2.69 Boston Massacre

2.70 Navigation Acts

2.71 Townshend Acts

2.72 Boston Tea Party

2.73 Trenton

2.74 Stamp Act

2.75 New York City

2.76 Intolerable Acts

2.77 Bunker Hill

2.78 *Common Sense*

2.79 Valley Forge

2.80 mercantilism

2.81 Second Continental Congress

2.82 America

2.83 Britain

2.84 Philadelphia

2.85 Thomas Jefferson

2.86 Samuel Adams

2.87 Fort Ticonderoga

2.88 Any order: Ethan Allen, Benedict Arnold

2.89 Either order: Gage, Howe, Cornwallis

2.90 a. Never attempted
 b. Retreated after he was unable to take Fort Stanwix
 c. He captured Ticonderoga but his advance was slowed by the local militia. His entire army was defeated at Saratoga.

2.91 He worked with guerrilla bands to draw out the British, inflict heavy losses and retreat. The losses eventually forced the British to withdraw.

2.92 Benedict Arnold

2.93 The federal government had no executive, no power to tax, control commerce or provide justice.

2.94 It was sold to pay off federal debts. The territories were allowed to organize into states with equal rights when they had enough people.

2.95 Shay's Rebellion

2.96 Saratoga

2.97 Cornwallis was trapped by the French fleet and a combination American/ French army and surrendered.

2.98 America was given independence and all the land east of the Mississippi

2.99 a. It would be by state in the Senate and by population in the House
 b. they counted as three-fifths of a person
 c. George Washington
 d. to allow free debate & compromise
 e. It could not be outlawed until 1807

2.100 executive, legislative, judicial

2.101 no Bill of Rights

2.102 Federalists

2.103 First ten amendments to the Constitution

2.104 essays in favor of the Constitution

2.105 Thomas Jefferson

2.106 XYZ Affair

2.107 1800

2.108 Whiskey Rebellion

2.109 Democratic-Republican

2.110 Louisiana Purchase

2.111 Lewis and Clark

2.112 Alexander Hamilton

2.113 Declaration of Neutrality

2.114 Federalist

2.115 Convention of 1800

2.116 Alien and Sedition Acts

2.117 *Marbury v. Madison*

2.118 Thomas Jefferson

2.119 John Adams

2.120 Federalist

2.121 Jay's Treaty

2.122 George Washington

2.123 They established our basic institutions, set up strong federal government and kept the new nation out of war

2.124 Tecumseh

2.125 *Constitution*

2.126 War Hawks

2.127 Barbary pirates

2.128 Canada

2.129 *Chesapeake-Leopard*

2.130 Embargo

2.131 Lake Erie

2.132 Democratic-Republican

2.133 Plattsburg Bay

2.134 impressment

2.135 Washington; Baltimore

2.136 Ghent

2.137 Aaron Burr

2.138 decreased

2.139 John Marshall

2.140 American System

2.141 Monroe Doctrine

2.142 Andrew Jackson; New Orleans

2.143 Era of Good Feelings

2.144 Napoleon was defeated and exiled

2.145 ✔

2.146

2.147 ✔

2.148 ✔

2.149 ✔

2.150

2.151

2.152 Government jobs were given to loyal supporters of the party regardless of qualifications. It led to corruption and poor quality work.

2.153 Adams won it in the House of Representatives because Henry Clay supported him. Then, Clay was made Secretary of State.

2.154 Missouri was admitted as a slave state, Maine as a free one, there was to be no more slavery north of 36° 30' boundary.

2.155 the cotton gin

2.156 South Carolina declared the tariff null and void in their state. Jackson threatened to use force. Clay arranged a compromise that lowered the tariff over ten years.

2.157 The Cherokee people were forced to move west, off of their land; many died on the journey.

2.158 It was closed when the president moved the federal funds out of it into "pet" banks.

2.159 A very high tariff proposed to embarrass Adams

2.160 He wanted all of it to 54° 40' but accepted a division with Britain at 49.°

2.161 A group of Texans held the fort for two weeks, inflicted heavy losses on the Mexicans and then were all killed.

2.162 Could states nullify federal laws

2.163 He sent soldiers south of the Neuces River into land claimed by Mexico, provoking a war.

2.164	d	2.181	Samuel Morse
2.165	g	2.182	shipping
2.166	c	2.183	Mormonism
2.167	a	2.184	mechanical reaper
2.168	f	2.185	abolitionist
2.169	e	2.186	Fugitive Slave Act
2.170	b	2.187	*Uncle Tom's Cabin*
2.171	Kansas-Nebraska Act	2.188	Winfield Scott
2.172	Compromise of 1850	2.189	Eli Whitney
2.173	Republican	2.190	Erie Canal
2.174	steamboat	2.191	Irish
2.175	Zachary Taylor	2.192	John Deere
2.176	railroads	2.193	Gadsden Purchase
2.177	Guadalupe Hidalgo	2.194	Samuel Slater
2.178	gold rush	2.195	hard surface roads
2.179	Industrial Revolution	2.196	textile
2.180	Second Great Awakening		

SECTION THREE

3.1	election of Abraham Lincoln	3.23	Charles Sumner
3.2	the beginning of the Civil War	3.24	hire a replacement
3.3	10%	3.25	Ulysses S. Grant
3.4	14th	3.26	sharecropping
3.5	Redeemers	3.27	abolitionist
3.6	Emancipation Proclamation	3.28	N
3.7	John Brown	3.29	S
3.8	Ulysses S. Grant	3.30	N
3.9	Dred Scott	3.31	S
3.10	Tenure in Office Act	3.32	S
3.11	14th	3.33	N
3.12	Lincoln-Douglas Debates	3.34	N
3.13	Alaska	3.35	N
3.14	Kansas	3.36	S
3.15	Carpetbaggers and Scalawags	3.37	S
3.16	Black Friday	3.38	N
3.17	13th	3.39	S
3.18	Hayes became president, Reconstruction was ended	3.40	S
3.19	hard money	3.41	S
3.20	Black Codes	3.42	N
3.21	15th	3.43	N
3.22	Whiskey Ring	3.44	S
		3.45	S

3.46	S
3.47	N
3.48	N
3.49	N
3.50	N
3.51	N
3.52	N
3.53	N
3.54	i
3.55	m
3.56	g
3.57	a
3.58	j
3.59	o
3.60	n
3.61	f
3.62	b
3.63	d
3.64	k
3.65	c
3.66	e
3.67	h
3.68	l
3.69	q
3.70	j
3.71	v
3.72	s
3.73	z
3.74	f
3.75	p
3.76	a
3.77	t
3.78	b
3.79	k
3.80	n
3.81	w
3.82	o
3.83	g
3.84	e
3.85	d
3.86	x

3.87	h
3.88	i
3.89	l
3.90	u
3.91	c
3.92	y
3.93	m
3.94	r
3.95	Low pay, no job protection, squalid slums, cities run by corrupt bosses
3.96	rich on the surface, corrupt underneath
3.97	repeating rifles, diseases, mobile army units and the destruction of the buffalo
3.98	kept all of it except for Cuba
3.99	Woodrow Wilson
3.100	Island hopping
3.101	U-boats; Pearl Harbor
3.102	Any two: free spending, illegal drinking, fads, prosperity
3.103	Stock Market Crash
3.104	Hundred Days
3.105	Denmark, Norway, Belgium, Netherlands, France
3.106	Germany invaded Poland
3.107	New Deal
3.108	John Pershing
3.109	the heir to the Austrian throne was assassinated
3.110	Scopes Monkey
3.111	Great Depression
3.112	Dwight D. Eisenhower
3.113	appeasement
3.114	Treaty of Versailles
3.115	Communist Revolution
3.116	18th
3.117	Stalingrad; Midway
3.118	MacArthur
3.119	the U.S. dropped two atomic bombs on Japan
3.120	Harding
3.121	Harry Truman

3.122 arms race, national pride, alliances

3.123 Herbert Hoover

3.124 World War II

3.125 North Africa; Italy; France

3.126 Manhattan

3.127 trench; *Blitzkrieg*

3.128 Calvin Coolidge

3.129 Battle of the Bulge

3.130 Holocaust

3.131 A conflict of ideas, economics, propaganda and intimidation between the U.S. and U.S.S.R. (1945-91).

3.132 nonviolent protest

3.133 *Brown v. Board of Education*

3.134 Peace Corps, Alliance for Progress, Nuclear Test Ban Treaty

3.135 Gulf of Tonkin Resolution

3.136 He made accusations about communists in the government and business.

3.137 The North attacked the South driving them back to the Pusan Perimeter. MacArthur sent an amphibious assault that drove the North back to near the Chinese border. Chinese soldiers counter attacked and it stalemated near the old border.

3.138 China became communist and the U.S.S.R. exploded an atomic bomb

3.139 legal inequality for Black Americans was finally ended

3.140 Missile sites were being built in Cuba. Kennedy blockaded the island to stop the delivery of missiles. The Soviets did not challenge the blockade and dismantled the sites.

3.141 James Earl Ray

3.142 Great Society

3.143 Civil Rights Act & Voting Rights Act

3.144 Berlin Wall

3.145 Fair Deal

3.146 U-2 Incident

3.147 Containment

3.148 Marshall Plan

3.149 NATO

3.150 Douglas MacArthur

3.151 Montgomery Bus Boycott

3.152 Dwight Eisenhower

3.153 "I Have a Dream"

3.154 Sputnik

3.155 Vietnam

3.156 Lee Harvey Oswald

3.157 communists

3.158 United Nations

3.159 Tet Offensive

3.160 NASA

3.161 b

3.162 c

3.163 d

3.164 e

3.165 a

3.166 f

3.167 c

3.168 b

3.169 a

3.170 f

3.171 b

3.172 c

3.173 d

3.174 a

3.175 e

3.176 d

3.177 f

3.178 c

3.179 f

3.180 inflation

3.181 Burglars who tried to bug the Democratic headquarters were connected to the White House staff. Nixon instructed them to hide their knowledge of the break-in. That was later proven using tapes he made in his office.

3.182 Revolts against communist rule occurred all over eastern Europe and all the governments eventually fell. Even the Berlin Wall was torn down.

3.183 Iraqi forces were driven out of Kuwait.

3.184 Fifty-two Americans from the Iran embassy staff were held for 444 days

3.185 1991

3.186 the Soviet invasion of Afghanistan

3.187 racial balance in all the schools in a district

3.188 social revolts of the 1960s

SELF TEST 1

1.01	d		1.015	Any order:
1.02	e			a. Rome
1.03	j			b. Greece
1.04	f			c. Jews
1.05	c			d. Christianity
1.06	g		1.016	✔
1.07	i		1.017	✔
1.08	h		1.018	
1.09	b		1.019	✔
1.010	a		1.020	

1.011   The Treaty was an agreement between Spain and Portugal to divide the newly discovered non-Christian lands of the world between them.

1.012   The Crusades were a series of campaigns to capture the Holy Land from the Turks. They brought Europe into contact with the goods and science of Asia which increased trade and knowledge in Europe.

1.013   The long route on land and sea was controlled on land by the Muslims and in Europe monopolized by the Italian cities.

1.014   A Portuguese prince who increased Europe's knowledge of ship building, navigation, and geography while organizing a trade route around Africa to Asia.

1.021	
1.022	✔
1.023	
1.024	✔
1.025	
1.026	✔
1.027	
1.028	
1.029	✔
1.030	true
1.031	false
1.032	true
1.033	true

SELF TEST 2

2.01	France	2.015	j
	The Gulf of St. Lawrence and the St. Lawrence River	2.016	f
		2.017	b
2.02	Netherlands	2.018	true
	Hudson River and the east coast of the U.S.	2.019	false
2.03	England	2.020	false
	Hudson Bay area, eastern Canada	2.021	true
2.04	France	2.022	true
	St Lawrence River, Great Lakes, east coast south to Massachusetts	2.023	false
		2.024	false
2.05	England		
	Newfoundland and U.S. east coast		
2.06	France		
	Mississippi River and tributaries from Lake Michigan to the Arkansas River		
2.07	France		
	Ohio River valley and Mississippi River		
2.08	g		
2.09	h		
2.010	d		
2.011	e		
2.012	i		
2.013	a		
2.014	c		

SELF TEST 3

3.01	Netherlands		3.027	Spain
3.02	England		3.028	France
3.03	France		3.029	France
3.04	Spain		3.030	England
3.05	Netherlands		3.031	
3.06	France		3.032	✔
3.07	England		3.033	
3.08	Spain		3.034	
3.09	Spain		3.035	✔
3.010	France		3.036	✔
3.011	c		3.037	✔
3.012	f		3.038	
3.013	g		3.039	✔
3.014	i		3.040	✔
3.015	a		3.041	Any two: lack of unity, inferior weapons, lack of immunity to European diseases, overwhelmed by the Europeans
3.016	d			
3.017	e			
3.018	j			
3.019	b		3.042	Company members were given large tracts of land in exchange for bringing over 50 settlers.
3.020	h			
3.021	France		3.043	Hudson River
3.022	England		3.044	Any two: autocratic government, government control of trade, land owned by wealthy landlords, no religious freedom
3.023	Spain			
3.024	France			
3.025	Spain			
3.026	France			

SELF TEST 1

1.01	Plymouth (Massachusetts)	1.025	b
1.02	Rhode Island	1.026	d
1.03	Connecticut	1.027	c
1.04	Maryland	1.028	d
1.05	Massachusetts	1.029	a
1.06	Connecticut	1.030	c
1.07	Georgia	1.031	false
1.08	Georgia	1.032	true
1.09	Maryland	1.033	true
1.010	Massachusetts	1.034	true
1.011	Connecticut	1.035	false
1.012	Massachusetts	1.036	true
1.013	New York	1.037	false
1.014	New Jersey	1.038	true
1.015	Pennsylvania	1.039	false
1.016	Virginia	1.040	false
1.017	Delaware		
1.018	Georgia		
1.019	South Carolina		
1.020	North Carolina		
1.021	c		
1.022	a		
1.023	b		
1.024	c		

SELF TEST 2

2.01	g		2.025	Middle
2.02	f		2.026	a. governor
2.03	i			b. council
2.04	j			c. assembly
2.05	h		2.027	Great Awakening
2.06	b		2.028	a. corporate
2.07	c			b. proprietary
2.08	d			c. self-governing
2.09	e		2.029	a. Congregationalists
2.010	a			b. Anglican
2.011	New England		2.030	New England Confederation
2.012	Southern		2.031	true
2.013	All		2.032	false
2.014	None		2.033	false
2.015	Middle		2.034	false
2.016	Middle		2.035	true
2.017	Southern			
2.018	New England			
2.019	None			
2.020	Southern			
2.021	New England			
2.022	Southern			
2.023	Middle			
2.024	New England			

SELF TEST 3

3.01	a. King William's War		3.020	Treaty of Paris
	b. Queen Anne's War		3.021	Ohio Valley
	c. King George's War		3.022	Anglican
	d. French and Indian War		3.023	Proclamation of 1763
3.02	Great Awakening		3.024	false
3.03	a. Puritans		3.025	false
	b. Quakers		3.026	true
	c. Catholics		3.027	false
	d. Separatists			
	e. Quakers		3.028	true
3.04	c		3.029	false
3.05	h		3.030	false
3.06	a		3.031	true
3.07	i		3.032	false
3.08	f		3.033	true
3.09	e			
3.010	b			
3.011	j			
3.012	d			
3.013	g			
3.014	New England Confederation			
3.015	Mayflower Compact			
3.016	Deism			
3.017	Fort Necessity			
3.018	Dominion of New England			
3.019	Quebec			

SELF TEST 1

1.01   f

1.02   i

1.03   h

1.04   a

1.05   j

1.06   d

1.07   c

1.08   e

1.09   g

1.010   b

1.011   A tax on all legal and public papers, must buy a stamp for them. It was the first direct tax on the colonies.

1.012   A tax on imports from Britain, revenue to be used to pay British officials, greater enforcement power given to customs officers, and threatened to dissolve New York assembly if it did not obey the Quartering Act

1.013   Mob in Boston threw things at British soldiers who fired on the crowd. Five people were killed.

1.014   Colonists disguised as Indians took the tea off three ships in Boston harbor and threw it in the water.

1.015   Boston harbor was closed, Massachusetts charter was changed so the officials were responsible to the king, town meetings were restricted, Boston put under military rule

1.016   French laws and religion in Quebec were protected. The colony's boundaries were expanded south into the Ohio Valley.

1.017   Americans fortified Breeds Hill near Boston, British attacked straight up the hill, Americans drove them back with heavy losses until forced to retreat because they ran out of powder

1.018   Any order:
    a. Stamp Act Congress
    b. boycotts
    c. mob action

1.019   mercantilism

1.020   Navigation

1.021   Declaratory

1.022   Sons of Liberty

1.023   Quartering

1.024   Sugar

1.025   Intolerable

1.026   Lexington

1.027   Ticonderoga

1.028   *Common Sense*

1.029   true

1.030   false

1.031   false

1.032   false

1.033   true

1.034   false

1.035   true

1.036   false

1.037   true

1.038   true

SELF TEST 2

2.01	c	2.026	France
2.02	m	2.027	Fort Ticonderoga
2.03	g	2.028	Philadelphia
2.04	l	2.029	mercantilism
2.05	n	2.030	Quebec Act
2.06	k	2.031	Stamp Act
2.07	o	2.032	Boston Tea Party
2.08	a	2.033	Any three: large, professional army; control of the seas; loyalists; unified government; good supplies; money to hire mercenaries
2.09	d		
2.010	h		
2.011	b		
2.012	i	2.034	true
2.013	j	2.035	false
2.014	e	2.036	true
2.015	f	2.037	false
2.016	Monmouth Courthouse	2.038	true
2.017	Trenton	2.039	true
2.018	Saratoga	2.040	false
2.019	Oriskany	2.041	true
2.020	King's Mountain	2.042	true
2.021	Valley Forge	2.043	true
2.022	Yorktown		
2.023	Long Island		
2.024	Charleston		
2.025	Camden		

SELF TEST 3

3.01	i		3.023	veto laws
3.02	g		3.024	nine
3.03	h		3.025	mercantilism
3.04	d		3.026	Any order:
3.05	j			a. Stamp Act Congress
3.06	b			b. boycotts
3.07	e			c. mob action
3.08	c		3.027	true
3.09	a		3.028	true
3.010	f		3.029	false
3.011	Benjamin Franklin		3.030	false
3.012	George Washington		3.031	false
3.013	Thomas Jefferson		3.032	true
3.014	James Madison		3.033	false
3.015	Benedict Arnold		3.034	true
3.016	Nathanael Greene		3.035	true
3.017	Lafayette		3.036	true
3.018	John Hancock			
3.019	George Rogers Clark			
3.020	Cornwallis			
3.021	Saratoga			
3.022	Any order:			
	a. executive			
	b. legislative			
	c. judicial			

SELF TEST 1

1.01	e	1.022	The Constitution did not specifically allow it.
1.02	c		
1.03	b	1.023	Any three:
1.04	g		set up basic government structures
1.05	h		kept the peace in early years
1.06	f		set up a strong financial base
1.07	j		loose construction of Constitution
1.08	a	1.024	Any three, any order:
1.09	d		a. giving aid to the Indians
1.010	i		b. seizing U.S. ships and cargo
1.011	Federalist		c. impressing American sailors
1.012	Democratic-Republican		d. holding forts in U.S. territory
1.013	pyramid	1.025	false
1.014	Whiskey Rebellion	1.026	false
1.015	none	1.027	false
1.016	XYZ Affair	1.028	true
1.017	Alien and Sedition Acts	1.029	false
1.018	Convention of 1800	1.030	true
1.019	"One out of many"	1.031	true
1.020	*Farewell Address*	1.032	true
1.021	Any order:	1.033	false
	a. pay debt at full value	1.034	false
	b. take over state debts	1.035	true
	c. National Bank		

136

SELF TEST 2

2.01	XYZ Affair	2.014	Any three:
2.02	War Hawks		set up government structure
2.03	Whiskey Rebellion		kept peace
2.04	Alien and Sedition Acts		set up strong financial base
2.05	Louisiana Purchase		loose construction of Constitution
2.06	Lewis and Clark	2.015	It was the first peaceful change of
2.07	Federalist		power between political parties.
2.08	Democratic-Republican	2.016	against the Barbary pirates
2.09	*Marbury v. Madison*	2.017	g
2.010	Embargo Act	2.018	a
2.011	Any order:	2.019	f
	a. impress American sailors	2.020	c
	b. aiding the Indians	2.021	b
	c. seizing U.S. ships and cargoes	2.022	j
2.012	No. (Any one of the following or	2.023	h
	others that the teacher approves):	2.024	i
	He kept the National Bank, made	2.025	e
	the Louisiana Purchase, passed and	2.026	d
	enforced the Embargo Act	2.027	a,b
2.013	The British ship *Leopard* fired on the	2.028	a,d,e
	Chesapeake killing several men and		
	damaging the ship to recover four		
	deserters.		

SELF TEST 3

3.01	capture Canada	3.013	Whiskey Rebellion
3.02	Any two:	3.014	*U.S.S. Constitution*
	keep part of Maine	3.015	Star-Spangled Banner
	Indian nation south of Great Lakes	3.016	d
	control of the Great Lakes	3.017	c
3.03	Any order:	3.018	g
	a. tariffs to protect industries	3.019	b
	b. National Bank	3.020	i
	c. improvements in transportation	3.021	h
3.04	Any two:	3.022	e
	impressment of sailors	3.023	j
	aid to the Indians	3.024	f
	seizure of ships and cargoes	3.025	a
3.05	Any two:	3.026	true
	pay debt at full value	3.027	false
	take over state debts	3.028	false
	National Bank	3.029	false
3.06	Monroe Doctrine	3.030	true
3.07	Battle of New Orleans	3.031	false
3.08	Washington	3.032	true
3.09	Democratic-Republican	3.033	false
3.010	New England	3.034	true
3.011	Hartford Convention	3.035	true
3.012	Era of Good Feelings		

SELF TEST 1

1.01	j		Defeated the Creek Indians as a militia general and the British at New Orleans as a U.S. army general.
1.02	d		
1.03	b		
1.04	g		
1.05	f	1.024	He prepared troops and supplies. He requested the Force Bill to authorize the army to collect the tariff in South Carolina. It was resolved by a compromise tariff that lowered the rates over several years.
1.06	i		
1.07	e		
1.08	c		
1.09	a		
1.010	h		
1.011	Tariff of Abominations	1.025	He wanted to force Jackson to veto or accept the charter believing that either one would hurt the president's popularity. Jackson did veto it and won the election anyway.
1.012	Missouri Compromise		
1.013	cotton gin		
1.014	Democrats		
1.015	National Republicans or Whigs		
1.016	John Quincy Adams		
1.017	Panic of 1837	1.026	Hundreds of people crowded in, breaking and tearing things. The crush forced Jackson to leave. The crowds left when punch was served on the lawn.
1.018	Spoils System		
1.019	Trail of Tears		
1.020	Specie Circular		
1.021	A state could nullify any federal law it believed was unconstitutional.	1.027	false
1.022	He was not popular and too honest to use government jobs to gain popularity. He was opposed at every turn by the Democrats angry over the defeat of Andrew Jackson.	1.028	true
		1.029	true
		1.030	true
		1.031	true
		1.032	false
1.023	He was the son of poor immigrants in Tennessee, orphaned as a young man. Became a successful lawyer, politician, and land speculator.	1.033	false
		1.034	false
		1.035	false
		1.036	false

SELF TEST 2

2.01 i

2.02 f

2.03 g

2.04 c

2.05 j

2.06 h

2.07 a

2.08 d

2.09 b

2.010 e

2.011 Any order:

  a. Daniel Webster

  b. Henry Clay

  c. John Calhoun

2.012 Mexican Cession

2.013 Fifty-four Forty or Fight

2.014 Remember the Alamo! or Remember Goliad!

2.015 Texas

2.016 California

2.017 Nullification

2.018 National Bank

2.019 Maine and Oregon

2.020 Taylor took a position in the disputed land north of the Rio Grande and was attacked by the Mexican army.

2.021 The campaign against Mexico City led by Winfield Scott

2.022 Santa Anna surrounded it. The defenders held him off for two weeks, then were all killed.

2.023 He was a popular military hero with no political experience.

2.024 U.S. received all of California and the land west of Texas, with borders set at the Rio Grande and Gila Rivers. U.S. paid $15 million to Mexico and took over Mexican debts to U.S. citizens.

2.025 Clay gave Adams the presidency in the House of Representatives vote in exchange for the position of Secretary of State.

2.026 They were split over the issue of slavery in the new lands.

2.027 The party could not agree on one of the major candidates and Jackson supported Polk.

2.028 It split into the Democrats and the Whigs (National Republicans).

2.029 j

2.030 g

2.031 i

2.032 d

2.033 a

2.034 h

2.035 f

2.036 b

2.037 e

2.038 c

SELF TEST 3

3.01	h	3.029	Alamo
3.02	d	3.030	Underground Railroad
3.03	b	3.031	Kansas-Nebraska
3.04	i	3.032	turnpikes
3.05	o	3.033	Potato Famine
3.06	p	3.034	Fugitive Slave Law
3.07	m	3.035	Republican
3.08	f	3.036	true
3.09	g	3.037	true
3.010	k	3.038	false
3.011	b	3.039	false
3.012	e	3.040	false
3.013	l	3.041	false
3.014	j	3.042	true
3.015	f	3.043	true
3.016	n	3.044	false
3.017	c	3.045	false
3.018	i	3.046	true
3.019	a	3.047	false
3.020	d	3.048	false
3.021	f	3.049	true
3.022	g	3.050	true
3.023	e	3.051	false
3.024	k	3.052	false
3.025	d	3.053	false
3.026	Industrial Revolution	3.054	true
3.027	Know-Nothing	3.055	true
3.028	Second Great Awakening	3.056	false

SELF TEST 1

1.01	b	1.022	Any two: ideals, military leaders, defensive position
1.02	g		
1.03	i	1.023	Any two: to keep their supply of cotton, to divide the U.S. democracy, to have a non-manufacturing trading partner, to support the Confederate aristocracy
1.04	j		
1.05	c		
1.06	f		
1.07	a		
1.08	h	1.024	Any two: Maryland, Delaware, Kentucky, Missouri
1.09	e		
1.010	d	1.025	true
1.011	Lecompton	1.026	true
1.012	Republican	1.027	false
1.013	Fort Sumter	1.028	true
1.014	Harper's Ferry	1.029	true
1.015	Lincoln-Douglas	1.030	true
1.016	Dred Scott	1.031	true
1.017	cotton	1.032	false
1.018	Kansas-Nebraska	1.033	true
1.019	South Carolina	1.034	true
1.020	Emancipation Proclamation		
1.021	Any four: farms, money, railroads, population, factories, resources, Black soldiers, navy, government		

SELF TEST 2

2.01	m	2.05	k
2.02	h	2.06	c
2.03	i	2.07	j
2.04	a	2.08	b

2.09	k
2.010	b
2.011	d
2.012	f
2.013	l
2.014	g
2.015	e
2.016	C
2.017	U
2.018	U
2.019	C
2.020	C
2.021	U
2.022	U
2.023	C
2.024	U
2.025	C
2.026	Kansas-Nebraska
2.027	Dred Scott
2.028	Emancipation Proclamation
2.029	Gettysburg
2.030	James Buchanan
2.031	Andersonville
2.032	disease
2.033	Appomattox Courthouse
2.034	John Wilkes Booth
2.035	South Carolina
2.036	Any two: military leaders, defensive position, ideals (early in the war)

2.037	He kept going after Lee hit him hard.
2.038	Any two:
	a. Emancipation Proclamation
	b. north sold them wheat and corn; north bought military supplies
2.039	Slavery could not constitutionally be ended where it existed, but it should not be allowed to spread.
2.040	Pro and anti-slavery forces fought with each other.
2.041	The north had more factories, farms, money, and better transportation to deliver what the army needed.
2.042	It was peaceful and reasonably normal in the midst of a civil war.
2.043	Older military tactics called for mass attacks which were mowed down by new rifles and artillery.
2.044	true
2.045	false
2.046	false
2.047	true
2.048	false
2.049	true
2.050	false
2.051	false
2.052	false
2.053	false

SELF TEST 3

3.01	Andrew Johnson	3.026	false
3.02	Alaska	3.027	true
3.03	Thirteenth	3.028	true
3.04	Boss Tweed	3.029	false
3.05	Crédit Mobilier	3.030	false
3.06	Fifteenth	3.031	true
3.07	Radical Reconstruction	3.032	true
3.08	Black Codes	3.033	true
3.09	Emancipation Proclamation	3.034	true
3.010	Fourteenth	3.035	true
3.011	Compromise of 1877	3.036	true
3.012	South Carolina	3.037	false
3.013	Vicksburg	3.038	true
3.014	Carpetbaggers	3.039	true
3.015	Fort Sumter	3.040	true
3.016	Abraham Lincoln	3.041	true
3.017	Dred Scott	3.042	true
3.018	Jefferson Davis	3.043	false
3.019	Robert E. Lee	3.044	true
3.020	Thaddeus Stevens	3.045	true
3.021	Stephen Douglas		
3.022	John Brown		
3.023	Ulysses S. Grant		
3.024	Stonewall Jackson		
3.025	Rutherford B. Hayes		

SELF TEST 1

1.01	g	1.024	immigrants were hard to organize, accepted low wages, and were used as strikebreakers
1.02	e		
1.03	a		
1.04	d	1.025	It was a federation of craft unions that focused on job issues.
1.05	i		
1.06	j	1.026	railroad, Homestead Act
1.07	h	1.027	They set rates high and often took the farmer's profit.
1.08	c		
1.09	b	1.028	They were getting higher wages than in Europe, did not complain, and seldom organized.
1.010	f		
1.011	trusts		
1.012	railroad	1.029	with strikebreakers, police, the army, and injunctions
1.013	Dawes Act		
1.014	New Immigration	1.030	They were proof of the success of the American way of life.
1.015	Haymarket Riot		
1.016	Laissez-faire	1.031	g
1.017	Homestead Act	1.032	c
1.018	Social Darwinism	1.033	i
1.019	Gilded Age	1.034	j
1.020	frontier	1.035	h
1.021	The cattle were raised cheaply on government grassland. They were driven to railroad junctions and taken to the cities for sale.	1.036	a
		1.037	e
		1.038	b
		1.039	d
1.022	stockholders own it, board of directors runs it	1.040	f
1.023	Union Pacific, Central Pacific		

SELF TEST 2

2.01	e	2.024	Knights of Labor
2.02	e	2.025	h
2.03	d	2.026	i
2.04	g	2.027	c
2.05	h	2.028	e
2.06	c	2.029	j
2.07	h	2.030	g
2.08	a	2.031	b
2.09	c	2.032	d
2.010	d	2.033	f
2.011	f	2.034	a
2.012	d	2.035	false
2.013	h	2.036	false
2.014	f	2.037	true
2.015	c	2.038	true
2.016	a. silver coinage	2.039	false
	b. inflation and debt relief	2.040	true
2.017	fight Indians	2.041	true
2.018	laissez-faire	2.042	true
2.019	Cuba's	2.043	false
2.020	Spanish-American War	2.044	true
2.021	Populist	2.045	false
2.022	tariff	2.046	false
2.023	spent it		

SELF TEST 3

3.01	Roosevelt		3.024	Populists
3.02	Taft		3.025	Plains Indians
3.03	Roosevelt		3.026	i
3.04	Wilson		3.027	h
3.05	Taft		3.028	j
3.06	Roosevelt		3.029	a
3.07	Wilson		3.030	e
3.08	Wilson		3.031	g
3.09	Taft		3.032	b
3.010	Roosevelt		3.033	c
3.011	Roosevelt		3.034	f
3.012	Wilson		3.035	d
3.013	Roosevelt		3.036	i
3.014	Taft		3.037	h
3.015	Roosevelt		3.038	c
3.016	city		3.039	j
3.017	muckrakers		3.040	e
3.018	*Cross of Gold*		3.041	g
3.019	Spanish-American War		3.042	b
3.020	Square Deal		3.043	a
3.021	Social Darwinism		3.044	f
3.022	railroads		3.045	d
3.023	Knights of Labor			

SELF TEST 1

1.01   e

1.02   f

1.03   g

1.04   j

1.05   b

1.06   a

1.07   h

1.08   c

1.09   d

1.010   i

1.011   alliances, arms race, national pride

1.012   Assassination of Archduke Ferdinand in Sarajevo, Bosnia

1.013   Both sides were protected in deep trenches and could rake unprotected attackers with machine gun and artillery fire.

1.014   submarine attacks

1.015   The invasion of neutral Belgium

1.016   A Communist Revolution

1.017   Influenza

1.018   Fourteen Points

1.019   Germany to pay the cost of the war and be crippled so as never to threaten France again

1.020   Any three: Poland, Yugoslavia, Czechoslovakia, Turkey, Austria, Hungary

1.021   League of Nations

1.022   He went on a national speaking tour to win the support of the American people for the treaty.

1.023   U.S.

1.024   observation

1.025   stay neutral

1.026   The British effectively blockaded the Central Powers who also could not get loans to pay for supplies.

1.027   Austria-Hungary and Serbia

1.028   They always destroyed the ship with its cargo and often killed the crew/passengers. Warships only seized cargo.

1.029   A note from the German Foreign Minister offering Mexico an alliance in exchange for recovering the American southwest.

1.030   Men

1.031   War Industries Board

1.032   Château-Thierry

1.033   zeppelins

1.034   Eddie Rickenbacker

1.035   Herbert Hoover

1.036   Meuse-Argonne

1.037   St. Mihiel

1.038   Dardanelles

1.039   Alvin York

1.040   *Lusitania*

SELF TEST 2

2.01	Roaring Twenties	2.029	d
2.02	stock market crash, 1929	2.030	e
2.03	Fundamentalists	2.031	Any five:
2.04	Prohibition		
2.05	agriculture	FERA:	gave money to the states for relief or jobs
2.06	submarine attacks	CWA:	temporary jobs
2.07	Bonus Army	HOLC:	low interest home loans
2.08	World War II	WPA:	public works projects
2.09	Hundred Days	NRA:	set up codes to encourage production
2.010	trench		
2.011	1933; 25	TVA:	built dams in Tennessee River Valley for electricity
2.012	John Pershing		
2.013	credit	AAA:	paid farmers not to farm
2.014	Scopes Monkey	CCC:	low-paying conservation jobs for young men
2.015	Archduke Ferdinand		
2.016	bank holiday	SEC:	monitor the stock market
2.017	organized crime	FDIC:	insure bank deposits
2.018	immigration	2.032	true
2.019	war	2.033	true
2.020	Teapot Dome	2.034	false
2.021	b	2.035	false
2.022	c	2.036	false
2.023	a	2.037	false
2.024	c	2.038	true
2.025	d	2.039	true
2.026	b	2.040	true
2.027	e	2.041	false
2028	e		

SELF TEST 3

3.01	e	3.023	Battle of the Bulge
3.02	a	3.024	Holocaust
3.03	j	3.025	Doolittle's Raid
3.04	d	3.026	stock market crash of 1929
3.05	b	3.027	German submarine attacks
3.06	f	3.028	North Africa; Italy; France
3.07	h	3.029	The assassination of Archduke
3.08	i		Ferdinand, Austria-Hungarian heir
3.09	c	3.030	Nazi invasion of Poland
3.010	g	3.031	It supplied the Allies with huge
3.011	Adolf Hitler		amounts of arms and supplies.
3.012	Franklin D. Roosevelt	3.032	the Roaring Twenties
3.013	Winston Churchill	3.033	He committed suicide.
3.014	Pearl Harbor	3.034	Soviet Union
3.015	appeasement	3.035	Atomic bombs dropped on
3.016	Britain		Hiroshima and Nagasaki
3.017	Japanese-Americans	3.036	false
3.018	blitzkrieg	3.037	false
3.019	Stalingrad	3.038	false
3.020	Midway	3.039	true
3.021	trench	3.040	false
3.022	island hopping		

SELF TEST 1

1.01	g	1.028	i
1.02	a	1.029	b
1.03	h	1.030	a
1.04	e	1.031	u
1.05	d	1.032	o
1.06	j	1.033	s
1.07	f	1.034	n
1.08	c	1.035	j

1.09   k

1.010   i

1.011   b

1.012   It was a conflict of ideas, economics, propaganda and intimidation between the U.S. and the Soviet Union that never became a hot war because of the fear of nuclear war.

1.013   Communism was to be contained, kept where it already existed by giving money, weapons and military assistance to stop communist aggression in free countries.

1.014   g

1.015   p

1.016   r

1.017   e

1.018   k

1.019   f

1.020   l

1.021   h

1.022   t

1.023   v

1.024   c

1.025   q

1.026   d

1.027   m

1.036   The North attacked driving the U.S. and the South back to the Pusan Perimeter. MacArthur landed at Inchon and drove the North back to near the Chinese border. Chinese soldiers then drove the U.S. back. The war stalemated at the 38th Parallel.

1.037   Repatriation, the communists wanted their prisoners of war returned by force. After Stalin's death, they agreed to voluntary repatriation with the right to visit those who refused to go.

1.038   It was a long, expensive war in favor of a corrupt government. Americans began to protest against it and many young men avoided the draft.

1.039   They set up communist regimes in their part of Europe and closed them off from the west. They also tried to gain control of Iran, Greece and Turkey.

1.040   The U.S.S.R. exploded an atomic bomb and the communists won the civil war in China.

SELF TEST 2

2.01   f

2.02   b

2.03   i

2.04   g

2.05   j

2.06   d

2.07   c

2.08   h

2.09   a

2.010   e

2.011   containment

2.012   Rosa Parks refused to sit in the back of the bus in Montgomery starting a bus boycott there

2.013   Booker T. Washington

2.014   "I Have a Dream"

2.015   inflation

2.016   Peace Corps

2.017   Berlin Wall

2.018   détente

2.019   Dwight Eisenhower

2.020   Gulf of Tonkin Resolution

2.021   Sputnik I, U.S.S.R.

2.022   I like Ike

2.023   Warsaw Pact

2.024   Alliance for Progress

2.025   Fair Deal

2.026   Spy planes showed missile bases being built in Cuba. Kennedy ordered the island blockaded to stop the missiles from being delivered. The Soviets did not challenge the blockade and agreed not to give Cuba missiles if the U.S. would not invade it.

2.027   Europe was not recovering from World War II. The U.S. offered aid to rebuild if Europe would draw up a plan. They did but the Iron Curtain nations were not allowed to participate. It was a great success.

2.028   The court ordered the school to integrate and nine Black students registered. The governor tried to stop them with the National Guard and a mob. Eisenhower sent in soldiers to escort the students.

2.029   Burglars were captured trying to bug the Democratic headquarters, one worked for Nixon's campaign. Several Nixon aides were involved and tried to cover it up. Recordings of Nixon's conversations proved he knew about the cover up. He resigned.

2.030   They peacefully disobeyed the laws by sitting, wading, walking and praying where they were not allowed. They also staged peaceful marches, registered voters and appealed to the courts.

2.031   A mass rebellion against traditional values like marriage and careers. protests of all kinds were common, especially against the Vietnam War. Caused increases in divorce, drug use and immorality.

2.032   *Plessy* said that Blacks and Whites could have "separate but equal" facilities. *Brown v. Board* said separate was inherently unequal and schools must integrate "with all deliberate speed."

SELF TEST 3

3.01	Watergate	3.021	k	
3.02	inflation	3.022	l	
3.03	Iran Hostage Crisis	3.023	b	
3.04	Beruit, Lebanon	3.024	m	
3.05	Iran-Contra Affair	3.025	n	
3.06	communism collapsed in Europe	3.026	a	
3.07	Persian Gulf War	3.027	e	
3.08	pardoned Nixon	3.028	d	
3.09	invasion of Afghanistan	3.029	f	
3.010	Camp David Accords	3.030	h	

3.011 Rosa Parks refused to sit in the back of the bus starting the Montgomery bus boycott

3.031
- a. ✔
- b.
- c. ✔
- d.
- e. ✔

3.012 Cuban Missile Crisis

3.32
- a. ✔
- b.
- c.
- d. ✔
- e. ✔
- f. ✔
- g.
- h.
- i. ✔
- j.

3.013 Marshall Plan

3.014 Western Bloc (Free or First World); Eastern Bloc (Communist or Second World); Third World

3.015 containment

3.33
- a. ✔
- b. ✔
- c. ✔
- d.
- e.
- f.
- g.
- h. ✔
- i. ✔
- j.

3.016 j

3.017 o

3.018 c

3.019 g

3.020 i

SELF TEST 1

1.01	h	1.018	Contract with America
1.02	b	1.019	cell phone/pager
1.03	f	1.020	Apple II
1.04	g	1.021	Social Security tax
1.05	d	1.022	Haiti
1.06	e	1.023	fax/facsimile
1.07	j	1.024	satellite
1.08	a	1.025	ENIAC
1.09	i	1.026	North Korea, China, Cuba
1.010	c	1.027	vacuum tubes

1.011 Improvements led to advances in communications, satellite usage, and medicine.

1.028 abortion

1.029 true

1.030 false

1.012 Machines can keep a body functioning after a person is dead.

1.031 false

1.032 true

1.013 Students protesting for greater freedom were attacked by the army, but the government denied that it happened.

1.033 false

1.034 true

1.035 true

1.014 Using a computer to visit information sites on the Internet.

1.036 false

1.037 true

1.015 People are encouraged to do what makes them happy (not what is right) and society does not condemn divorce.

1.038 true

1.039 true

1.040 false

1.016 e-mail

1.041 true

1.017 NAFTA

SELF TEST 2

2.01	a		2.033	a
2.02	p		2.034	k
2.03	r		2.035	d
2.04	m		2.306	m
2.05	j		2.037	l
2.06	y		2.038	e
2.07	s		2.039	f
2.08	b		2.040	i
2.09	h		2.041	o
2.010	u		2.042	r
2.011	e		2.043	p
2.012	v		2.044	Massachusetts (Bay)
2.013	c		2.045	Georgia
2.014	d		2.046	France
2.015	n		2.047	Spain
2.016	o		2.048	France
2.017	t		2.049	Britain
2.018	w		2.050	Jamestown (Virginia)
2.019	l		2.051	New York
2.020	x		2.052	Rhode Island
2.021	f		2.053	Delaware and Pennsylvania
2.022	q		2.054	south
2.023	k		2.055	Maryland
2.024	g		2.056	Plymouth
2.025	i		2.057	It ended the era of compromise by allowing slavery north of the Missouri Compromise line.
2.026	c		2.058	Any two: generals, location, possible allies
2.027	h		2.059	A change from agriculture and handcrafts to industry and machine manufacturing.
2.028	n			
2.029	q			
2.030	b			
2.031	g			
2.032	j			

SELF TEST 3

3.01	m		3.035	x
3.02	aa		3.036	g
3.03	g		3.037	k
3.04	f		3.038	c
3.05	p		3.039	i
3.06	o		3.040	h
3.07	d		3.041	a
3.08	dd		3.042	t
3.09	t		3.043	e
3.010	s		3.044	q
3.011	e		3.045	j
3.012	x		3.046	f
3.013	h		3.047	l
3.014	b		3.048	r
3.015	q		3.049	m
3.016	cc		3.050	o
3.017	j		3.051	s
3.018	a		3.052	n
3.019	v		3.053	u
3.020	u		3.054	d
3.021	c		3.055	War of 1812
3.022	z		3.056	Civil War
3.023	l		3.057	World War I
3.024	r		3.058	Revolutionary War
3.025	k		3.059	French and Indian War (Seven Years War)
3.026	n			
3.027	w		3.060	Mexican War
3.028	bb		3.061	Persian Gulf War
3.029	y		3.062	Korean War
3.030	i		3.063	Great Depression
3.031	b		3.064	Spanish-American War
3.032	p		3.065	World War II
3.033	w		3.066	Vietnam War
3.034	v		3.067	Take off 1 point for every 4 mistakes

1.	d	31.	tobacco
2.	t	32.	Portugal
3.	r	33.	Henry the Navigator
4.	a	34.	Italy
5.	i	35.	sea dogs
6.	k	36.	Northwest Passage
7.	e	37.	Grand Banks
8.	q	38.	Huguenots
9.	l	39.	fur
10.	n	40.	St. Augustine
11.	f	41.	true
12.	s	42.	false
13.	m	43.	false
14.	g	44.	true
15.	b	45.	true
16.	o	46.	true
17.	p	47.	true
18.	j	48.	false
19.	c	49.	false
20.	h	50.	false
21.	d		
22.	b		
23.	c		
24.	d		
25.	d		
26.	b		
27.	c		
28.	c		
29.	b		
30.	b		

1.	f	26.	Massachusetts
2.	g	27.	Massachusetts
3.	m	28.	Maryland
4.	i	29.	Rhode Island
5.	o	30.	Connecticut
6.	n	31.	New York
7.	j	32.	New Jersey
8.	h	33.	Georgia
9.	k	34.	North Carolina
10.	c	35.	South Carolina
11.	l	36.	true
12.	d	37.	true
13.	a	38.	false
14.	b	39.	false
15.	e	40.	true
16.	fishing	41.	true
17.	wheat	42.	true
18.	rice	43.	true
19.	proprietary	44.	false
20.	Congregationalists	45.	true
21.	Mayflower Compact		
22.	Georgia		
23.	French and Indian War		
24.	Proclamation		
25.	Quaker		

1. g

2. c

3. d

4. j

5. a

6. b

7. i

8. e

9. f

10. h

11. Congress would be made of two houses: representation in the Senate would be by state and in the House by population

12. Cornwallis was trapped on Chesapeake bay by the French navy and a combined America/French army. He was surrounded and surrendered his whole army.

13. Britain was arrogant after winning the Seven Years War and deeply in debt. They wanted some revenue from the colonies and greater control over them.

14. Stamp Act: tax on legal and public documents by way of a stamp

    Quebec Act: French kept their laws and expanded into the Ohio Valley

    Quartering Act: troops kept at the expense of the colonists

Townshend Acts: tax on British imports

Intolerable Acts: close Boston harbor, change charter

15. A rebellion of debtors in Massachusetts. It scared many people into supporting a stronger government.

16. Lexington

17. Lafayette

18. Rochambeau

19. Monmouth

20. Cornwallis

21. Stuben

22. Ticonderoga

23. Camden

24. Saratoga

25. Trenton

26. Second Continental Congress

27. Stamp Act Congress

28. Articles of Confederation

29. Confederation Congress

30. Constitution of the U.S.

31. Second Continental Congress

32. First Continental Congress

33. Articles of Confederation

34. Constitution of the U.S.

35. Second Continental Congress

1.	P	21.	h
2.	C	22.	e
3.	R	23.	g
4.	R	24.	d
5.	C	25.	i
6.	P	26.	b
7.	C	27.	a
8.	R	28.	c
9.	R	29.	f
10.	C	30.	j
11.	Florida	31.	b
12.	XYZ Affair	32.	c
13.	Federalist	33.	a
14.	Great Seal	34.	d
15.	Louisiana Purchase	35.	c
16.	Alien and Sedition Acts	36.	b
17.	tariffs	37.	a
18.	Era of Good Feelings	38.	b
19.	McHenry	39.	c
20.	Hartford Convention	40.	b

1.	d	26.	e
2.	f	27.	o
3.	c	28.	j
4.	a	29.	f
5.	a	30.	m
6.	b	31.	b
7.	b	32.	a
8.	h	33.	l
9.	i	34.	n
10.	e	35.	c
11.	f	36.	k
12.	g	37.	g
13.	b	38.	i
14.	b	39.	d
15.	f	40.	h
16.	Missouri Compromise	41.	true
17.	Compromise of 1850	42.	false
18.	Trail of Tears	43.	true
19.	Manifest Destiny	44.	false
20.	"Fifty-four Forty or Fight"	45.	true
21.	Clipper Ships	46.	true
22.	Erie Canal	47.	false
23.	the tariff	48.	false
24.	Spoils system	49.	true
25.	Oregon Trail	50.	false

1. b; the south had better generals and the south could not break the blockade <u>because</u> the north had more resources

2. b; corruption and share cropping had other causes beyond Reconstruction and it was white power that had the longest negative effect

3. c; disease killed more than bullets

4. a; without the issue of slavery the rest would not have mattered

5. c; this was the prime Republican issue

6. Appomattox Courthouse

7. Gettysburg

8. Emancipation Proclamation

9. Robert E. Lee

10. John Wilkes Booth

11. Thirteenth

12. Alaska

13. Gettysburg Address

14. Ulysses S. Grant

15. William T. Sherman

16. Black Codes

17. Bleeding Kansas

18. Dred Scott

19. Fourteenth

20. Crittendon Compromise

21. He kept going after Lee mauled his army.

22. He was acquitted by one vote.

23. It had more resources to get supplies and a better transportation system to deliver them.

24. It gave Lincoln a victory he needed to publish the Emancipation Proclamation.

25. The south passed Black Codes and elected Confederate leaders to Congress.

26. e

27. h

28. j

29. a

30. d

31. i

32. g

33. c

34. b

35. f

1. Gilded Age

2. silver coinage

3. Spanish-American War

4. Any order:

   a. Homestead Act

   b. railroad

5. Federal Reserve Act

6. railroads

7. He supported a revolution in Panama and signed a treaty with the new government.

8. Cattle was raised cheaply on government grassland then driven to railroad junctions and shipped to cities.

9. Forbid political "donations" from government employees, established Civil Service Commission to test people for certain government jobs

10. R, T, W

11. G, M

12. C, W

13. C

14. A

15. M

16. R

17. R, T

18. T

19. W

20. Big Stick

21. New Immigration

22. William J. Bryan

23. Billion Dollar Congress

24. Sherman Anti-Trust

25. Model T

26. Civil War veterans (G.A.R.)

27. 1890

28. *Maine*

29. Open Door

30. true

31. false

32. true

33. true

34. false

35. false

36. false

37. true

38. false

39. false

BONUS:

40. Grange, Farmer's Alliance, Populists

1. h
2. i
3. e
4. j
5. g
6. c
7. b
8. a
9. d
10. f
11. Nazi invasion of Poland
12. Atomic bomb
13. German submarine attacks
14. Fourteen Points
15. Communist Revolution
16. World War II
17. 25%
18. Treaty of Versailles
19. bank
20. Fundamentalists
21. false; change *Herbert Hoover* to *Woodrow Wilson*
22. false; change *kamikaze* to *blitzkrieg*
23. true
24. false; change *Mao Tse-tung* to *Chiang Kai-shek*
25. false; change *Great Britain* to *Pearl Harbor*

26. true
27. true
28. false; change *a depression* to *an arms race*
29. false; change *France* to *Belgium*
30. false; change *Pas-de-Calais* to *Normandy*
31. Their code of honor would not let them surrender so they often fought to the death.
32. They were New Deal agencies created to help Americans during the Great Depression.
33. Stock prices rose on speculation based on credit purchases.
34. He blindly trusted his friends who took advantage of their power in a series of scandals.
35. The British attacked from Egypt. Another American led force landed in Morocco, trapping them in the middle.
36. The death of about six million people in Nazi concentration camps.

1. Marshall Plan
2. Warsaw Pact
3. Persian Gulf War
4. Vietnam War
5. Cuban Missile Crisis
6. Iran Hostage Crisis
7. "I Have a Dream"
8. inflation
9. Gulf of Tonkin Resolution
10. Watergate
11. Korean War
12. Iran-Contra Affair
13. Berlin Wall
14. Peace Corps
15. NATO
16. U.S. policy during the Cold War–communism was to be contained where it already existed by fighting it in free nations.
17. A conflict of ideas, propaganda, economics and intimidation between the U.S. and Soviet Union from 1945 to 1991. The fear of nuclear destruction kept it from ever being a hot war.
18. A war fought during the Cold War to stop communism in one country. It was not allowed to spread any further than that nation or area.

19. Reforms by Gorbachev in the 1980s in the Soviet Union. *Perestroika* was economic reform while *glasnost* was greater freedom of speech.
20. A "thaw" in the Cold War in the 1970s. It included SALT I & II, Nixon's visit to the Soviet Union and greater trade.
21. Communism collapsed all over eastern Europe as people demonstrated for more freedom. The Berlin Wall was destroyed.
22. Black people would peacefully challenge the laws by going where they were not allowed to be and staying. They also marched, filed lawsuits and registered voters.
23. Americans lost confidence in their government, the military and themselves, particularly in their ability to defeat communism.
24. f
25. h
26. i
27. j
28. d
29. b
30. c
31. e
32. g
33. a

1.	13	21.	f
2.	4	22.	e
3.	15	23.	i
4.	12	24.	p
5.	20	25.	r
6.	14	26.	a
7.	10	27.	j
8.	8	28.	n
9.	11	29.	q
10.	18	30.	g
11.	6	31.	b
12.	19	32.	o
13.	5	33.	t
14.	16	34.	c
15.	7	35.	l
16.	9	36.	k
17.	17	37.	d
18.	3	38.	h
19.	1	39.	m
20.	2	40.	s

51. George Washington
52. Theodore Roosevelt
53. Lyndon Johnson
54. Andrew Jackson
55. Harry Truman
56. Abraham Lincoln
57. Jimmy Carter
58. Thomas Jefferson
59. Woodrow Wilson
60. John Adams
61. Andrew Johnson
62. Warren Harding
63. George Bush
64. John Kennedy
65. Franklin Roosevelt

66.	i	71.	f
67.	h	72.	b
68.	a	73.	d
69.	g	74.	c
70.	j	75.	e

41. ended the era of compromise before the Civil War
42. this harsh treaty set up World War II by its treatment of Germany
43. convinced many Americans to seek independence from Britain
44. last major battle of the Revolution, convinced the British to grant independence
45. a lot of activity that brought hope and confidence to a nation devastated by the Great Depression
46. book that portrayed the evils of slavery and turned the north against it
47. put Europe in permanent contact with the Americas
48. ended 100 years of legal inequality for Black Americans after the Civil War
49. triggered the Great Depression
50. Congress gave the president free reign to act in Vietnam, Johnson used it to send in more and more soldiers, getting the nation deeper into that conflict

Bonus: Take off 1 point for every 2 mistakes

Grover Cleveland, 1885-1889
Benjamin Harrison, 1889-1893
Grover Cleveland, 1893-1897
William McKinley, 1897-1901
Theodore Roosevelt, 1901-1909
William Howard Taft, 1909-1913
Woodrow Wilson, 1913-1921
Warren Gamaliel Harding, 1921-1923
Calvin Coolidge, 1923-1929
Herbert Clark Hoover, 1929-1933
Franklin Delano Roosevelt, 1933-1945
Harry S. Truman, 1945-1953
Dwight David Eisenhower 1953-1961
John Fitzgerald Kennedy, 1961-1963
Lyndon Baines Johnson, 1963-1969
Richard Milhous Nixon, 1969-1974
Gerald Rudolph Ford, 1974-1977
James Earl Carter, Jr., 1977-1981
Ronald Wilson Reagan, 1981-1989
George Herbert Walker Bush, 1989-1993
William Jefferson Clinton, 1993-2001
George Walker Bush, 2001-2009
Barack Hussein Obama, 2009-

1. a
2. j
3. c
4. g
5. h
6. i
7. j
8. f
9. b
10. l
11. k
12. d
13. e
14. a
15. e
16. England
17. Spain
18. Portugal
19. France
20. Netherlands
21. Spain
22. Spain
23. Spain
24. France
25. France
26. England

27. Spain
28. England
29. Spain
30. France
31. Britain
32. Spain
33. France
34. Spain
35. Netherlands
36. Marco Polo
37. Crusades
38. tobacco
39. Any order: Rome, Greece, Jews, Christianity
40. Jamestown
41. Asia
42. Henry the Navigator

1. Pennsylvania
2. Rhode Island
3. New York
4. Virginia
5. Pennsylvania
6. Maryland
7. Connecticut
8. Delaware
9. Maryland
10. Georgia
11. North Carolina
12. Massachusetts
13. Georgia
14. New Jersey
15. South Carolina
16. French and Indian War
17. Pontiac's War
18. Glorious Revolution
19. King William's War
20. Bacon's Rebellion
21. King Phillip's War
22. French and Indian War
23. Queen Anne's War
24. French and Indian War
25. Pontiac's War

26. King George's War
27. French and Indian War
28. Great Awakening
29. Mayflower Compact
30. Dominion of New England
31. a. governor
    b. council
    c. assembly
32. Proclamation of 1763

1. m

2. f

3. n

4. s

5. t

6. g

7. q

8. e

9. j

10. r

11. k

12. b

13. c

14. o

15. i

16. a

17. h

18. l

19. p

20. d

21. Any order:

    a. Stamp Act Congress

    b. boycotts

    c. mob action

22. Valley Forge

23. a. France

    b. Benjamin Franklin

24. Boston Tea Party

25. Any order:

    a. trial by jury

    b. presumed innocent

26. Olive Branch Petition

27. Britain was deeply in debt from the Seven Years (French and Indian) War.

28. Any two:

    representation in Congress, counting slaves, the slave trade

29. Articles of Confederation

30. *The Federalist*

31. Any two: location; quality of commanders; soldiers' ability to shoot accurately; righteous cause; tough and capable people; wide spaces to withdraw; Britain had to defeat a large territory and uncooperative people; foreign allies

32. Any order:

    a. executive

    b. judicial

    c. legislative

1.	g	29.	Alexander Hamilton
2.	p	30.	Aaron Burr
3.	i	31.	John Marshall
4.	h	32.	Andrew Jackson
5.	t	33.	John Adams
6.	x	34.	Henry Clay
7.	w	35.	William Henry Harrison
8.	a	36.	true
9.	l	37.	true
10.	s	38.	false
11.	m	39.	false
12.	v	40.	true
13.	f	41.	false
14.	j	42.	false
15.	k	43.	false
16.	o	44.	true
17.	u	45.	true
18.	r	46.	true
19.	q	47.	true
20.	y	48.	true
21.	n	49.	true
22.	b	50.	false
23.	c	51.	false
24.	d	52.	true
25.	e	53.	false
26.	Thomas Jefferson	54.	false
27.	George Washington	55.	false
28.	James Monroe		

1.	r	29.	j
2.	h	30.	t
3.	n	31.	s
4.	s	32.	q
5.	d	33.	f
6.	i	34.	i
7.	o	35.	b
8.	q	36.	h
9.	k	37.	d
10.	t	38.	o
11.	c	39.	k
12.	b	40.	g

13. a

14. p

15. g

16. f

17. m

18. j

19. e

20. l

21. e

22. m

23. r

24. c

25. n

26. p

27. l

28. a

41. Any three:
treatment of the insane, women's rights, working conditions, education, slavery, temperance, prison and punishment, debt laws

42. Any order:
a. Democratic
b. Whig (National Republicans)

43. a. Kansas-Nebraska Act
b. Stephen Douglas

44. Andrew Jackson

45. Any one:
land speculation, credit from unstable banks, Jackson's economic policies (close National Bank, *Specie Circular*)

46. gold rush

1.	k	32.	William T. Sherman
2.	o	33.	William Seward
3.	h	34.	Ulysses S. Grant
4.	r	35.	John Crittendon
5.	t	36.	The south thought Britain would need their cotton, but it needed northern wheat and corn more and found other sources for cotton.
6.	d		
7.	a		
8.	c		
9.	l	37.	Congress passed the Tenure of Office Act which forbade the president to dismiss his cabinet members. He was impeached when he did so and acquitted by one vote.
10.	s		
11.	n		
12.	b		
13.	q		
14.	m	38.	Rifles and artillery had become more accurate but old military tactics called for mass attacks that were suicidal against the new weapons.
15.	e		
16.	f		
17.	i		
18.	j	39.	The south had better generals, fought for the ideal of independence and only had to fight a defensive war. A draw would be a southern victory.
19.	g		
20.	p		
21.	Abraham Lincoln		
22.	James Buchanan	40.	It is a policy that all money is gold, silver, or paper backed by a certain value of one of those. It shrinks the money supply which can make a depression worse.
23.	Ulysses S. Grant		
24.	Andrew Johnson		
25.	Rutherford B. Hayes		
26.	Robert E. Lee		
27.	Jefferson Davis	41.	true
28.	David Farragut	42.	true
29.	Thadeus Stevens	43.	false
30.	Stonewall Jackson	44.	false
31.	Stephen Douglas	45.	false

1. j
2. t
3. n
4. d
5. c
6. b
7. m
8. r
9. l
10. p
11. g
12. s
13. e
14. q
15. f
16. o
17. k
18. i
19. h
20. a
21. Corporate monopolies and abuse of power
22. Populist
23. He supported a revolution in Panama and signed the treaty with the new government.
24. city
25. It was a time of rapid industrialization, progress, wealth, and invention on the surface with exploitation, corruption, and social problems underneath.

26. Roosevelt and Taft split the Republican vote
27. f
28. j
29. m
30. d
31. l
32. k
33. n
34. h
35. g
36. e
37. o
38. i
39. b
40. c
41. a
42. false
43. false
44. false
45. true
46. true
47. false
48. true
49. false
50. true
51. false
52. true
53. true

1. s

2. q

3. g

4. m

5. d

6. c

7. o

8. w

9. p

10. y

11. i

12. x

13. j

14. v

15. t

16. e

17. u

18. f

19. b

20. r

21. a

22. h

23. k

24. l

25. n

26. Dwight D. Eisenhower

27. Woodrow Wilson

28. Douglas MacArthur

29. Adolf Hitler

30. Winston Churchill

31. John Pershing

32. Herbert Hoover

33. Benito Mussolini

34. Joseph Stalin

35. Archduke Ferdinand

36. false; change *blitzkreig* to *trench*

37. false; change *50%* to *25%*

38. true

39. false; change *became a free and stable democracy* to *paid for the war and could never threaten France again*

40. false; change *the Soviet Union* to *Great Britain*

41. false; change *Japanese* to *Chinese*

42. true

43. true

44. false; change *cigarettes* to *alcohol*

45. false; change *Sicily* to *North Africa* **or** change *first* to *second*

Alternate Test Key 809

1. h; Ford
2. f; Truman
3. g; Nixon
4. o; Johnson
5. m; Bush
6. c; Kennedy
7. j; Bush
8. d; Johnson
9. k; Truman
10. a; Carter
11. e; (a) Truman (b) Eisenhower
12. b. Eisenhower
13. n; Bush
14. i; Reagan
15. p; Kennedy
16. Cold War
17. Civil Rights Movement
18. Containment
19. Marshall Plan
20. inflation
21. Mikhail Gorbachev
22. *détente*
23. Peace Corps
24. separate but equal
25. Cambodia
26. communism
27. false
28. false
29. true
30. true
31. false

Alternate Test Key 810

1. Congress could not tax or control commerce, no executive or federal courts
2. Many people left because of the strict religious control of the Puritans
3. An arms race, competing alliances and national pride
4. The U.S. could not win the war and were supporting a corrupt and unpopular government
5. They established our institutions, set up a strong government and kept the new nation out of war
6. Impressment of U.S. sailors, interference with trade and the desire to take Canada
7. A conflict of ideas, economics, intimidation and propaganda between the U.S. and U.S.S.R. (1945-91)
8. A change from agriculture and handcrafts to industry and machine manufacturing.
9. Over use of credit, problems in the farm economy, bad distribution of wealth and stock market speculation

Alternate Test Key 810 (cont)

10.	They were defending their homes, only had to survive to win, had better generals and hope of allies		35.	a
11.-30	Subtract one point for a single item out of order, not for all that follow it.		36.	q
			37.	u
			38.	v
			39.	h
11.	3		40.	e
12.	20		41.	n
13.	19		42.	x
14.	2		43.	b
15.	4		44.	f
16.	6		45.	s
17.	12		46.	g
18.	18		47.	t
19.	16		48.	w
20.	11		49.	j
21.	1		50.	d
22.	14		51.	p
23.	10		52.	k
24.	5		53.	m
25.	7		54.	y
26.	9		55.	o

27.	17
28.	8
29.	13
30.	15
31.	l
32.	r
33.	c
34.	i

Bonus: Take off 1 point for every 2 mistakes

Grover Cleveland, 1885-1889
Benjamin Harrison, 1889-1893
Grover Cleveland, 1893-1897
William McKinley, 1897-1901
Theodore Roosevelt, 1901-1909
William Howard Taft, 1909-1913
Woodrow Wilson, 1913-1921
Warren Gamaliel Harding, 1921-1923
Calvin Coolidge, 1923-1929
Herbert Clark Hoover, 1929-1933
Franklin Delano Roosevelt, 1933-1945

Harry S. Truman, 1945-1953
Dwight David Eisenhower 1953-1961
John Fitzgerald Kennedy, 1961-1963
Lyndon Baines Johnson, 1963-1969
Richard Milhous Nixon, 1969-1974
Gerald Rudolph Ford, 1974-1977
James Earl Carter, Jr., 1977-1981
Ronald Wilson Reagan, 1981-1989
George Herbert Walker Bush, 1989-1993
William Jefferson Clinton, 1993-2001
George Walker Bush, 2001-2009
Barack Hussein Obama, 2009-